Pyrer

Roger Büdeler

Pyrenees 1

Central Spanish Pyrenees:
Panticosa to Benasque

50 selected valley and mountain walks in the central Spanish Pyrenees

With 91 colour photos, 50 small walking maps to a scale of 1:25,000,
1:50,000 and 1:75,000 and a contextualising map to a scale of 1:500,000

ROTHER · MUNICH

Cover photo:
Añisclo canyon and the Marboré massif with Punta de las Olas,
Soum de Ramond and Monte Perdido

Frontespiece (page 2):
Faja de la Tormosa in Valle de Pineta

All photos by the author

Cartography:
walking maps to a scale of 1:25,000 / 1:50,000 / 1:75,000
© Bergverlag Rother GmbH, Munich
Contextualising map to a scale of 1:500,000 / 1:800,000
© Freytag & Berndt, Vienna

Translation:
Gill Round

1st edition 2003
© Bergverlag Rother GmbH, Munich

ISBN 3-7633-4821-2

Distributed in Great Britain by Cordee, 3a De Montfort Street, Leicester
Great Britain LE1 7HD, www.cordee.co.uk

Foreword

The central Spanish Pyrenees in the province of Huesca form the most varied mountain and valley scenery in the whole of the Pyrenees with the Parque Nacional de Ordesa y Monte Perdido as the central section. The famous National Park was given world cultural heritage status in 1997 by Unesco and offers the walker an enormous wealth of striking natural images and unusual contrasts in the landscape. The fabulous canyons and mountain basins are to a large extent unique, together with high plateaus covered with a myriad of flowers, softly undulating mountain ranges and the dramatically distorted limestone masses of the three-thousanders with Monte Perdido as a superb summit objective. No less fascinating and varied are the neighbouring valleys around Benasque and Panticosa. Countless mountain lakes, huge granite peaks, bizarre limestone chains and delightful high pastures characterise the scenery and, of course, the huge glacial massif of Maladeta in the Posets Maladeta nature reserve with Pico de Aneto as the highest peak in the whole of the Pyrenees.

The paths on offer to the walker are as varied as the diversity of landscape: leisurely valley paths or steep rocky paths, mule paths with wonderful views or adventurous ascents up to a summit, old bridle paths or spectacular ledges which are to a certain extent 'suspended between mountain and valley'. There's a new and exciting view of the mountains constantly being displayed and the area is not yet showing the signs of the organised walking experience and the stylisation of nature for tourists.

In spite of the clear increase in numbers of visitors, mass tourism in the central Spanish Pyrenees has still, to a considerable degree, been kept within reasonable limits. This can also be seen in the towns where there's some provision for tourists, and many of them have preserved their beautiful old town centres and retained their quaint character. There are plenty of quiet corners, isolated paths and opportunities for the solitary enjoyment of nature, even during the six week high season when the streams of visitors limit themselves to just a few highlights of the area.

The 50 routes described in this walking guide hopefully offer a representative selection of walks that will do justice to the varied facets of the landscape and suit the different needs and capabilities of the walker. Enjoy your days in the central Spanish Pyrenees!

Summer 2003   Roger Büdeler

Contents

Tourist tips

Use of the guides
The walks are divided into four areas from west to east according to the main valleys: Valle de Tena / Valle Bujaruelo; Ordesa y Monte Perdido National Park; Valle de Bielsa / Valle de Gistaín and Posets-Maladeta National Park. The most important information you need for the walk is contained in a fact-file and there's a short description of the landscape before each walk is outlined. The line of the route is marked on a little colour map. All the destinations of the walks, starting points and key areas and named landmarks along the way can be found in the index. There is also a contextualising map showing the location of all the walks.

Grade
The waymarking and maintenance of the hiking trails in the Pyrenees cannot be compared to those in the Alps. The exceptions are the red and white marked GR paths (Gran Recorrido) and the yellow and white PR paths (Pequeño Recorrido) and, of course, the frequently used classic routes along well-trodden paths. Apart from that you have to follow the more or less well-placed cairns, but be aware that this kind of waymarker can easily be eroded by stonefall, animals or snow. You also need to find your way across terrain sometimes where there are no paths and animal tracks can take you off course. The best requirement, therefore, is a good sense of

Valle Ordesa: information centre for the national park.

direction and this is even essential on a few routes in the moderate and higher grades. Since this walking area is in the high mountains in the south, you also need to take into consideration the climatic conditions. The heat and intensity of the sun should never be underestimated in summer, especially on long hikes where there's no shade. An adequate provision of water is essential for every walk and in high summer, springs dry up quickly. The numbers of the walks are colour-coded to help you assess the grade.

BLUE
Easy and safe walk on obvious paths. The length of the route is within reasonable limits and the gradient is predominantly moderate; greater variations in height are spread over a longer stretch.

RED
Moderately difficult routes which place higher demands on energy and fitness because of their length and the steep, more sustained gradients. Walks numbered in red can be along narrow paths and include exposed sections, as well as sections of easy scrambling which are clearly indicated. Some experience of walking in the mountains, sure-footedness and good route-finding skills are essential.

BLACK
Difficult hikes which should only be undertaken by experienced and fit mountain walkers with sure-footedness, a head for heights and a good sense of direction. Together with very big variations in height, strenuous and steep gradients and exposed areas of path, there might also be sections of easy climbing (grade I maximum).

Dangers
Most of the walks go along obvious and well-made paths and often GR or PR trails. Walks in the high mountains can lead through demanding terrain with indistinct paths. Exposed paths, steep scree slopes, or climbing over rocks and boulders, are given special mention. On walks along balconies (fajas) at the foot of steep rock faces you should be prepared for the possibility of stonefall. The *faja* walks should be avoided at all cost in conditions of rain, snow and ice. Stones and boulders in the wild streams are frequently unstable and slippery and so particular care should be taken as you cross them. As always in the mountains, you can expect swift changes in the weather conditions in the Pyrenees and you can encounter snow, fog and icy winds on the summit. Do not be misled by the beautiful weather and high summer temperatures at the starting point and be sure to take the necessary precautions when it comes to carrying adequate protection for all conditions.

In high summer there's a chance of localised thunderstorms late in the afternoon, which then subside in the early evening again. Always make a

Clavijas de Carriata (Walk 18).

relatively early start when going on one of the long walks.

Equipment

The usual walking gear – sturdy shoes, mountain clothing and possibly walking poles – is necessary on all walks. It should be comfortable enough if it's hot, but at the same time give adequate protection against the rain, cold and wind. Make sure you take sufficient water and food with you since there are no huts available on most of the walks and springs might have dried up.

Always carry a map too, (at least 1:40,000), so that you are able to follow the description of the path and identify the mountains.

Maps

Up to a few years ago the availability of maps was poor. Various publishers have recently brought out some new maps, but they are still inaccurate at times and contain serious mistakes in places. In addition, there's a tendency to mark topographical names and terms in the local dialect which, for the walker with no knowledge of the language, can be confusing. A map is recommended for every walk, i.e. the best available at the present time, but even this will not be free of mistakes.

Walking times

The walking times given in this guide are, of course, only the approximate times. The actual time taken depends on the fitness of the walker and the weather conditions. The times given are based on an average tempo and do not take account of stops. Routes with difficult route-finding are timed more generously.

Refugios (mountain huts)

Only a very few of the *refugios* in this walking region are of the type with which you are familiar in the Alps. Most of the *refugios* that you pass on the walks are more or less intact shepherds' huts which are only usable as a shelter or in an emergency, if you can get into them at all. There are also self-catering huts which usually offer room for 4 to 6 people, but are mostly

Refugio de Góriz: starting point for mountain walks around the Marboré massif.

limited to one room with an open fire, table and benches. So for an overnight stop you need to take food, a sleeping bag and mat with you. Many of the *refugios* on long distance walks or at strategic starting points have such a small capacity that you are advised also to take a tent, giving you the flexibility to sleep out in the open if you need to. The tourist information office will give you more information. Each walk contains a short description of the *refugios* on the way. Since there are so few staffed *refugios* in the whole of this walking region not many walks offer you the opportunity of finding a meal and a place to spend the night. And even then you must be prepared for only a limited service. Always book ahead if you want a meal and to stay overnight. Very few of the staffed huts are open all year round and some huts, which are usually self-catering, are open between May and September.

Staffed huts open all year round are:

- ■ Refugio de Respomuso (2200 m) ✆ 974.49.02.03 (Valle de Tena)
- ■ Refugio Casa de Piedra (1638 m) ✆ 974.48.75.71 (Valle de Tena)
- ■ Refugio de Góriz (2200 m) ✆ 974.34.12.01 (Valle de Ordesa)
- ■ Refugio de San Nicolás de Bujaruelo (1338 m) ✆ 974.48.64.12 (Valle de Bujaruelo)
- ■ Refugio de Pineta (1200 m) ✆ 974.34.11.47 (Valle de Pineta)
- ■ Refugio de Éstos (1895 m) ✆ 974.55.14.83 (Valle de Benasque)

■ Refugio de la Renclusa (2140 m) ☏ 974.55.14.90 – 974.55.21.06 (Valle de Benasque)

Getting there

It is advisable to hire a car to drive to the starting points. There are only bus connections between the larger towns on the edge of the walking region and the timetable for these is very limited. Since the mountain valleys have only been developed with surfaced roads to a limited extent, many of the starting points are only accessible along tracks, which, if walked, would make the approaches longer than the walking routes themselves. The condition of these access routes is often not the best, but all of the tracks to the starting points mentioned here in the walk descriptions are accessible in a normal car and with the necessary care and attention. Only approximate times are given for longer journeys along tracks. The approach to the most frequented valleys has recently been regulated during Easter week (Semana Santa) and from 1st July until 15th October. There are special limits of access by car for the following valleys (as of 2001):

■ Valle de Ordesa: pay car park before Torla. From here there's a shuttle bus which leaves every 15 minutes from 8.00 onwards to the Pradera de Ordesa. The outward journey is in operation daily between 6.00 and 19.00 (18.00 in September and October); the last bus is at 22.00 (21.00 in September and 20.30 in October).

View from Tozal del Mallo into the Valle de Ordesa.

- Cañón de Añisclo: the drive through the Desfiladero de las Cambras is one-way from the National Park boundary. You have to return via Buerba and Puyarruego.
- Valle de Benasque: the road from Hospital de Benasque to La Besurta is closed off. A shuttle bus leaves the car park just before Hospital de Benasque daily at 5.00, 5.30, 7.15 and at least every half hour between 8.00 – 21.00. The track into the Valle de Vallibierna to the Refugio de Coronas is closed off. A shuttle bus leaves La Senarta daily at 6.15, 7.45, 9.15, 11.00 and 15.15. Return journeys are at 13.00, 16.00 and 18.00.

Alterations and up-to-date timetables can be obtained from the tourist offices.

Protection of the environment

The generally accepted rules of behaviour for the protection of the environment should be observed in the whole of the walking region. In addition to these, special rules and regulations for the Parque Nacional de Ordesa y Monte Perdido and the Parque Posets-Maladeta have been issued and they are strictly controlled in these areas. Please obtain further information from the tourist offices.

Tips for long distance walkers

Pyrenean violets.

Several GR paths go across this walking region, the principal one being the GR 11 (Senda Pirenaica) which crosses the whole of the Spanish Pyrenees from the Mediterranean to the Atlantic. It runs through the central region of this area mainly parallel to the central ridge of the mountains while the GR15 and GR19 run more along the periphery. The GR paths offer very beautiful opportunities for multi-day walks which can also be combined with the well-maintained and waymarked PR paths to form extremely pleasant round walks. There are also some delightful walks over the border onto the French side and several routes in this guide go over passes from where you can link up with paths into the French valleys (eg Walks 7,

Puerto de Marcadau, 2545m (Walk 7).

10, 12, 13, 32, 33, 34, 39, 44, 46). Highly recommended is the three-day walk in the Parque Posets-Maladeta which links the three Refugios of Viadós, Angel Orús and Estós.

Abbreviations

GR (Sendero de Gran Recorrido)	Long distance path
PR (Sendero de Pequeño Recorrido)	Pyrenees hiking trail

Spanish – English vocabulary for mountain walkers

abrigo	shelter	gorga	gorge
aigüeta	stream, river	gradas	ledges, steps
arista	mountain ridge	ibón	lake
barranco (Bco.)	gully, gorge	lago	lake
barrera	barrier	llano	plain (meadows, pastureland)
borda	hut, barn		
cabaña	(shepherds') hut	mirador	viewpoint, look out
camino	road, path		
cañon	canyon	peña	rock, crag, cliff
carretera	road	pico	peak, summit
cascada	waterfall	pista	track, roadway
chorro	cascade, waterfall	plano	plain
		pluviómetro	rain gauge
circo	valley basin, cirque	puente	bridge
		puerto	mountain pass
clavijas	iron bolts	punta	peak, summit
collado	hill, pass	refugio	mountain hut
collet (Catalan)	hill, pass	río	stream, river
cresta	mountain ridge	salto	waterfall
cuello	hollow, pass	sendero	waymarked hiking trail
cueva	cave		
embalse	reservoir	surgencia	spring
ermita	hermitage	torrente	mountain stream, torrent
estany (Catalan)	lake		
faja	balcony, ledge	tuca	summit, peak
fuente	spring, fountain	valle	valley
glera	scree		

Walking in the central Pyrenees

Geography

The Pyrenees extend between the Mediterranean and the Atlantic in a relatively straight line. The highest peaks of this 400km long chain of mountains are Aneto (3408m), Posets (3369m) and Monte Perdido (3355m). They lie in the region of the central Pyrenees which comprise the largest part of the Aragon Pyrenees. Several important massifs are concentrated between the Valle de Tena in the west and the valley of the Río Noguera Ribagorzana in the east like Balaïtous, Marboré, Posets-Llardana and Maladeta with a large number of three-thousanders. The peaks on the border with France form a continuous barrier with only a few breaks. Four main valleys running from north to south divide the mountain region and in the Ordesa and Monte Perdido National Park the relief is characterised by several large canyons with an east-west course. The whole area is abundant with water and is crossed by numerous rivers and streams. While only the Lago de Marboré is of importance in the National Park there is a wealth of wonderful high mountain lakes in the neighbouring massifs.

Geological history of the central Pyrenees

The central Pyrenees have developed out of two rock complexes which date from different geological periods. The original material consists of a huge mass of granite, metamorphic rock and hard limestone which was uplifted 250 million years ago for the first time during the formation of the Variscan mountains. There resulted from this uplift a symmetrically built mountain base which ran, to a large extent, in a straight line and is referred to as the central axis of the Pyrenees. This old central ridge started to sink in the Cretaceous period as a result of a reversal of the lifting process while the central Mediterranean (Thetys) flooded more and more of the mainland. There was a deposition of layers of marine sediment which, in the course of time, has been transformed into limestone. Consequently this younger rock complex formed a thick layer on top of the primary rock.

After a relatively stable phase of tectonic inactivity the alpine mountain formation of the Pyrenees began 35 million years ago. The original mountain base was lifted again and with it the huge overlying deposit of limestone on the seabed which in the meantime found itself again on the retreat.

During this folding phase there were large cracks in the rigid primary rock and in the younger limestone blanket, which peeled off in large masses from the underground and was displaced to the north and south. As it did so, many uplifted layers were created which sometimes ended up lying mirror-inverted on top of one another. The extreme faults and cracks of the younger rock are characteristic of the area of the present day Parque

Rock structures on the way to the Puerto de Marcadau (Walk 7).

Nacional de Ordesa y Monte Perdido. The Parque Posets-Maladeta, on the other hand, is built predominantly from the rock of the original mountain base so that essentially granite, crystalline slate and primary limestone are dominant here.

Huge fractures in the rock were caused by the enormous pressure of the uplift and displacement. They formed the starting point for the erosion by ice and water. The formation of huge glaciers began 2 million years ago and covered large areas of the central Pyrenees. The most important ice masses, up to 800m thick, lay in the massifs of the Marboré, Posets and Maladeta and flowed from the summit regions right down into the valleys. A magnificent example of the distinctive glacial erosion is the U-shaped Valle de Ordesa with its terraced valley slopes. With the melting of the glaciers numerous lakes have been left behind, especially in the larger valley basins of the massif. Today the only remaining glaciers worth mentioning are in the Maladeta massif and on Monte Perdido.

The erosive effect of the water is displayed most effectively in the limestone region of the central Pyrenees. Expansive limestone landscapes have been created here, considerable cave systems and large subterranean water conduits of which the Forau de Aiguallut in the Parque Posets--Maladeta is well-known. Many of the cracks and crevices remaining in the surface of the earth's crust have been eroded by water to become deep clefts in which

Beech wood on the way to the Llanos de la Larrí (Walk 31).

there are ridges and gorges hidden with a fantastic wealth of bizarre and intricate shapes.

Vegetation

There's a diversity of vegetation extending from the Mediterranean area up to the high alpine climatic region. In the more humid micro-climate you will find pine, ash, mountain acorn, birch, elm, hazelnut and aspen. Holm oaks are widespread which can grow up to an altitude of 1000m, and beech which are often encountered together with silver firs at altitudes between 1200 and 1700m. The black pine is widespread in the sub-alpine altitudes and above that, the uncinate pine dominates up to the tree line at 2300m. Here there is also an abundance of rhododendron and gorse. The box tree thrives at various altitudes and frequently forms a dense vegetated undergrowth.

The flowers in the alpine meadows and pastures form a marvellous display, especially in early summer. Crocus, alpine violets, anemones, (Pulsatilla vulgaris) pasque flowers, cowslips and buttercups begin to bloom in May, followed by various species of gentian and daffodils as well as yellow iris, which are in blossom from June or July onwards. You also come across edelweiss from time to time. The alpine rose appears in August. Two endemic species grow in the shelter of the rock and steep crags: the

Pyrenean violet which prefers damp and shady places, and the Pyrenean saxifrage.

Fauna

The Pyrenean ibex has, for a long time, been gradually decimated so that there are only a few still living in the area around the Faja de Pelay in the Valle de Ordesa. On the other hand, chamois are quite frequent and, similarly, you often see marmots in the high valleys, and sometimes dwarf stoats. You will also find fox, badgers, doormice, stone martins, wild cats, genets and wild boar, but you seldom see fish otters by the mountain streams. The central Pyrenees are a real birds' paradise and more than 125 species have been recorded. Regular companions in the mountains are alpine jackdaws and the red-beaked alpine chough which is quite striking with its raucous call and aerobatics. Amongst the birds of prey you will find, together with goshawks and buzzards, several species of eagles and vultures of which the lammergeier is an extremely rare visitor. Only 60 pairs nest in the whole of the Pyrenees, and 40 of them are supposed to live in the National Park area. On the other hand, you will often see griffon vultures in their dozens circling high above the crags.

It's not a rarity for you to come across snakes on your walks. Together with harmless adders there are also a few poisonous snakes like the heavily decimated asp viper and the very rare horned viper (cerastes). Representing the amphibians, as well as the salamander you might find the Pyrenean mountain newt which lives in the cold streams near to springs. It is also called *guardafuentes* (guardian of the spring).

National parks and nature reserves

The Parque Nacional de Ordesa y Monte Perdido was already established in 1918 by royal decree. The conservation area at that time only consisted of the Río Arazas valley. The purpose of creating a national park was to promote the protection of the unique mountain landscape and of the Pyrenean ibex. In 1982 the small surface area of little more than 2,000 hectares was increased to 15,600. This area includes the whole of the Monte -Perdido massif and the valleys of Ordesa and Escuaín as well as the Cañón de Añisclo. It shares the border in the north with the French Parc National des Pyrénées.

The Parque Posets Maladeta was founded in 1994. With a surface area of more than 30,000 hectares, it includes both the large massifs of Posets-Lllardana and Maladeta to the west and east of the Benasque valley. Together with the general rules for environmental sensitivity in the mountains, there are special regulations in the two nature reserves which should be respected without fail. Make yourself familiar with the necessary regulations at the tourist offices and from the information boards of the park authorities.

Canyoning

This mountain sport enjoys great popularity. There are numerous gorges at all grades of difficulty. In the larger towns you will find tour organisers offering guided excursions.

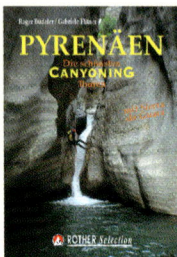

Paragliding

The Valle de Benasque is a well-known and ideal region for paragliders. The world championships take place there every two years. The launching point is Castejón de Sos where there are also paragliding schools.

Caving

The limestone massif of the central Pyrenees contains a great number of caves many of which have not yet been explored. The more famous and best mapped caves are the ice caves of Gruta de Casteret in the Marboré massif (not accessible) as well as the big cave system of Fuentes de Escuaín and Arañonera, the latter with a length of 34km and just under 1200m in height difference.

You can only visit the caves in the National Park with a permit from the park authorities. Tour operators offer guided cave visits to smaller caves. So, for example, a very pleasant excursion combines the traverse of the Cueva de Aso (see Walk 21) with a descent into the Río Aso gorge.

Climbing

There are numerous graded climbing routes which have been established at all grades. You can find climbing schools in Panticosa, Bielsa and Benasque, amongst others. Climbing inside the National Park needs a permit and information can be obtained from the park authorities.

Mountainbiking

Many tracks offer excellent opportunities with wonderful views for cycling trips where you can cover a variety of distances and heights. As the starting point of many of the walks is reached along a track, it makes a very pleasant excursion if you combine cycling with walking. Sports shops rent out mountain bikes.

Skiing

There are ski lifts and prepared slopes in Formigal and Panticosa in the Valle de Tena as well as in Cerler in the Valle de Benasque. There are opportunities for ski-touring in wonderful surroundings in the whole of the area, but multi-day trips are limited since there's a dearth of mountain huts. The track from Nerín to Cuello Arenas is open in winter so that you have an excellent starting point for going on ski tours right in the heart of the National Park.

Wild water rafting

Canoeing and rafting are widespread, and the Esera, Cinca, Cinqueta and Ara rivers are the most popular rivers for this sport.

The Río Ara is particularly well-known because, with easy to very difficult sections, it caters for everyone. If you prefer still water you will find rowing a boat on the valley reservoirs a pleasant alternative. The Embalses de Mediano and El Grado south of Aínsa should be mentioned here in particular. You can hire a boat from sports shops and tour organisers.

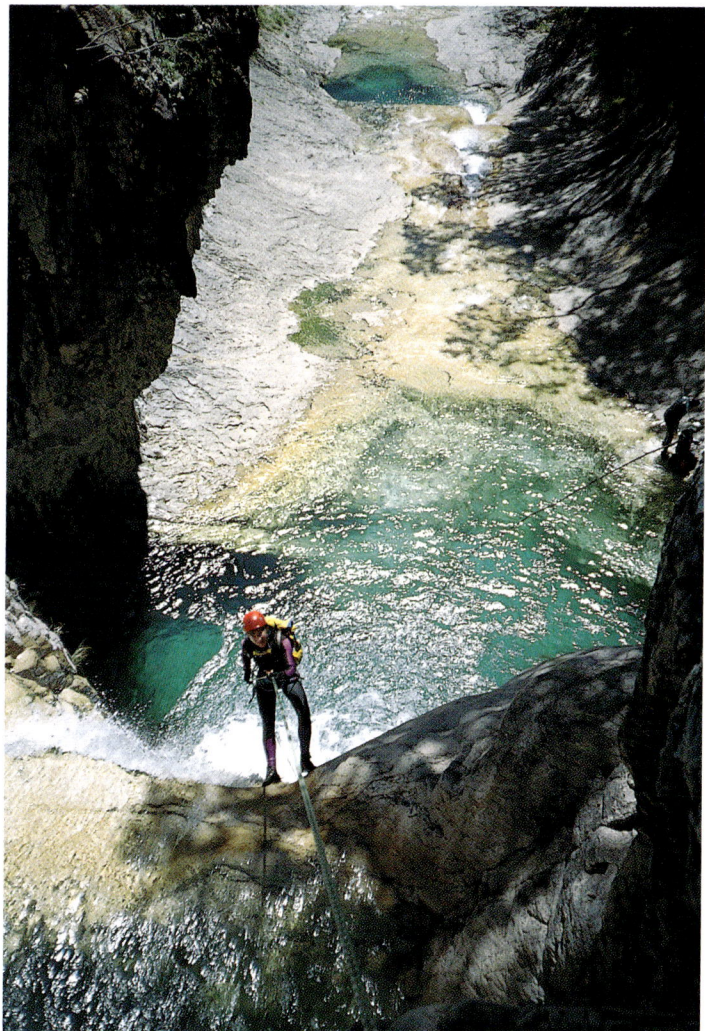

Canyoning in the Garganta de Escuaín.

Information and addresses

Information
Tourist organisation for the Provinz Huesca: Oficina de Información de Turismo, Huesca, Coso Alto, 23; ✆ 974-225778. Local tourist information in the main valleys (usually only open in summer): Panticosa ✆ 974.48.72.48; Torla ✆ 974.48.61.25; Broto ✆ 974.48.60.02; Boltaña ✆ 974.50.20.43 (open all year round); Aínsa ✆ 974. 50.07.67; Bielsa ✆ 974. 50.11.27; Benasque ✆ 974.55.12.89 (open all year round). Ordesa y Monte Perdido National Park: Centro visitante del Parque Nacional; ✆ 974.24.33.61. The visitors' centre can be found at the start of Valle de Ordesa. Posets Maladeta nature reserve ✆ 974.55.20.66.

Mountain rescue
Guardia Civil: Socorro en Montaña: ✆ 062 (mobile telephone: 974-062). S.O.S.Aragón: ✆ 112

Campsites and wild camping
There are campsites in the main valleys and the more important side valleys. Most of them are open between May and October, a few of them until December or even all year round.

In the designated wildlife reserves and in the National Park camping in the wild is forbidden. But from a certain altitude upwards walkers are allowed to put up a tent overnight. The individual areas in the National park have the following regulations: Ordesa from 2100m, Añisclo from 1800m, Escuaín from 1800m, Pineta from 2500m. Further information can be obtained from the tourist offices.

Climbing on the Faja-de-las-Flores walk.

Local holidays, national holidays and festivals
The main holiday periods are Easter week (Semana Santa) and from 15th July up until the end of August. There are a great number of local festivals, many of them in honour of a patron saint. Every village organises its own fiesta with food and dancing, sometimes sev-

eral a year. There are also festivals based in the larger towns which are observed nation-wide. The Morisma in Aínsa is very famous where they re-enact the expulsion of the Moors. Spectacular and atmospheric music festivals with international guests take place annually in Lanuza (Festival de las Culturas Pirineos Sur) in Valle de Tena and in Aínsa castle (Festival Internacional de Música).

'Las Navatas' on the Rio Cinca.

Opening times

Shops are open usually Monday to Saturday between 10.00 and 14.00 and 17.00 and 20.00 (frequently on Sunday too, in the high season). Banks are open between 9.00 and 14.00 Monday to Friday.

Climate

May and June, as well as September and October, are the nicest months due to warm temperatures and settled weather conditions. In high summer the weather is very hot from the middle of July and in August. You can expect quickly developing thunderstorms in the afternoon, especially in the second half of July and the first half of August. An Indian summer in September can frequently offer settled weather. From the second half of October the weather can be really changeable with autumnal rain and the first snow in the high mountain regions, and then in November and December, it can be exceptionally mild again. The real winter occurs in the months of January to March with snowfalls and cold temperatures.

Best time to go

The walker will find the best conditions in early and late summer as well as in autumn, i.e. from May until the beginning of July and the end of August until the middle of October. Most of the flowers are in bloom in May and June and in October you can enjoy the splendid autumn colours in the forests.

Telephone

Code for Spain 0034; local code for Provinz Huesca 974.

Walking and mountaineering clubs

Federación Aragonesa de Montañismo (FAM), Albareda 7, 50004 Zaragoza, ✆ 976-227971; E-Mail: fam@pirineos.net; http://www.pirineos.net/fam

Weather forecast

Daily updated recorded information for the Aragon Pyrenees region: ✆ 906.36.53.22

Bielle 1973 · Aste-Béon · Ferrières · Sère-en-Lavedan · Ayzac-Ost · Ourdon · Ayros-Arbouix · 1746 · Beaudé · l'Esponne

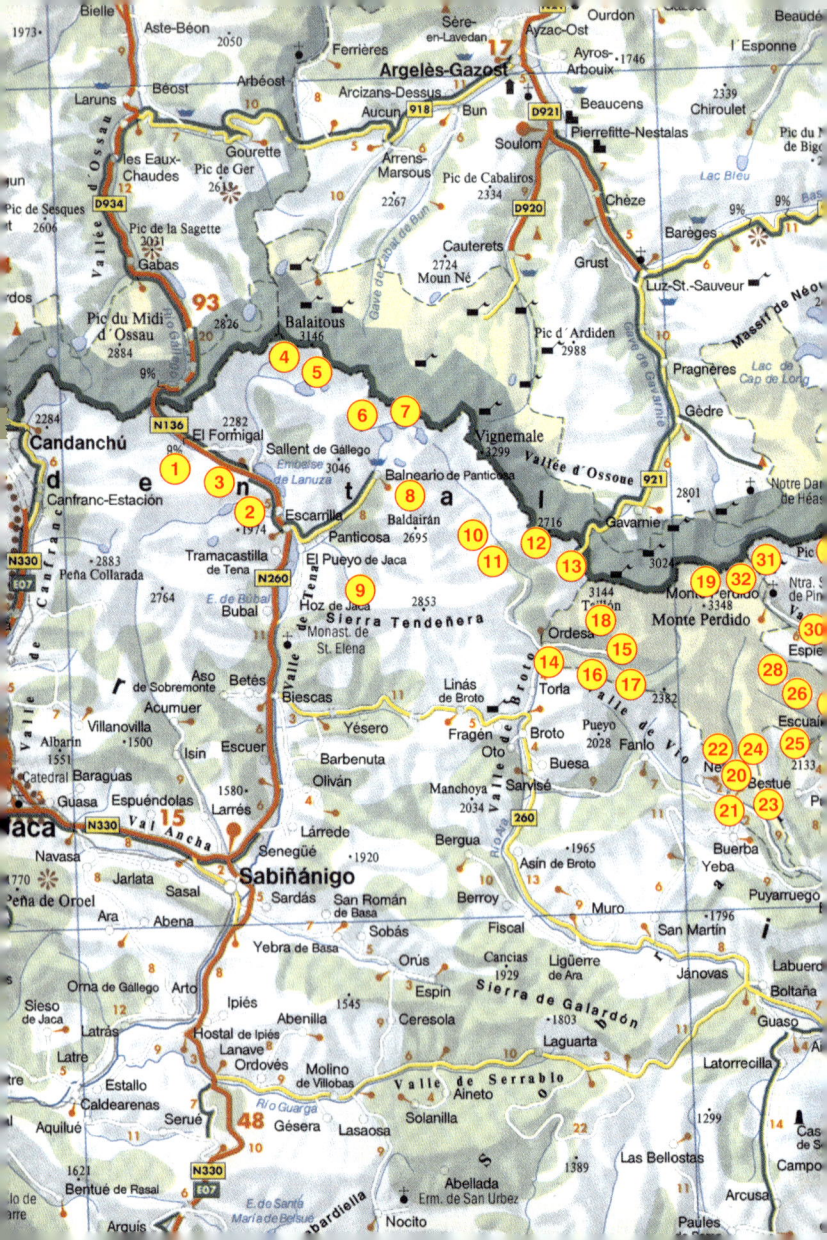

Arbéost · 2050 · Argelès-Gazost · Arcizans-Dessus · Beaucens · Chiroulet · 2339 · Pic du N de Big

les Eaux-Chaudes · Gourette · Pic de Ger 2613 · Aucun · 918 · Bun · Pierrefitte-Nestalas · D921 · Lac Bleu · Barèges · 9% · 9%

D934 · Pic de la Sagette 2031 · Gabas · Arrens-Marsous · Pic de Cabaliros 2334 · D920 · Chèze · Luz-St.-Sauveur · Massif de Néou

Pic de Sesques 2606 · Vallée d'Ossau · Cauterets 2724 · Moun Né · Grust · Pragnères · Lac de Cap de Long · Gèdre

93 · Pic du Midi d'Ossau 2884 · 2826 · Balaïtous 3146 · Pic d'Ardiden 2988 · 2801 · Notre-S de Héas

Candanchú · N136 · El Formigal · 2282 · Sallent de Gállego · Vignemale 3299 · Vallée d'Ossoue · 921 · Monte Perdido · Ntra.S de Pin

Canfranc-Estación · Embalse de Lanuza 3046 · Balneario de Panticosa · 2716 · Gavarnie · 3024 · Monte Perdido 3348 · 3144 · Tuquen · Pic

Peña Collarada 2883 · Escarrilla · Baldairán · Panticosa 2695 · 2974 · Tramacastilla de Tena · N260 · El Pueyo de Jaca · Ordesa

2764 · E. de Búbal · Bubal · Hoz de Jaca · Monast. de St. Elena · Sierra Tendeñera 2853 · Linás de Broto · Valle de Broto · Torla · 2382

Aso de Sobremonte · Betès · Biescas · Yésero · Fragén · Broto · Pueyo 2028 · Fanlo · Escuai

Acumuer · Villanovilla · 1500 · Escuer · Barbenuta · Oto · Buesa · Ne · 2133 · Bestué

Albarín 1551 · Isín · Oliván · Manchoya 2034 · Sarvisé · 260 · Buerba

Catedral Baraguás · Guasa · Espuéndolas · Larrés · 1580 · Lárrede · Bergua · Asín de Broto · 1965 · Yeba · Puyarruego

Jaca · N330 · Val Ancha · Senegüé · 1920 · Berroy · Muro · San Martin · 1796

Navasa · Jarlata · Sasal · Sabiñánigo · San Román de Basa · Fiscal · Jánovas

Peña de Oroel · Ara · Abena · Sardás · Sobás · Cancias 1929 · Ligüerre de Ara · Labuerd · Boltaña

Orna de Gállego · Arto · Yebra de Basa · Orús · Espín · Sierra de Galardón · Guaso

Sieso de Jaca · Latrás · Ipiés · Abenilla · 1545 · Ceresola · 1803 · Laguarta · Latorrecilla

Latre · Hostal de Ipiés · Lanave · Ordovés · Laguarta · 1299

Estallo · Caldearenas · Serué · Molino de Villobas · Valle de Serrablo · Aineto · Cas de S

Aquilué · 48 · Gésera · Lasaosa · Solanilla · Las Bellostas · Campo

1621 · Bentué de Rasal · N330 · E07 · E. de Santa María de Belsué · Arbardiella · Nocito · Abellada · Erm. de San Urbez · Arcusa

Arquis

champan • 1595
Hèches
Nistos
Seich
de-Comminges
Bertren
Malvezie
Izaut-
de-l'Hôtel
Aspet

35
e
Marie-
champan
D929
Ilhet
Troubat
Mauléon-Barousse
Créchets
Ste-Marie
Ourde
Saléchan
Fronsac
D33
Saint-Pé-d'Ardet
Arguenos
Juzet-d'Izaut
Sengouagnet
Pic de Cagire
1912
1608
Henne-
618
14%
9%

Sarrancolin
Espiadet 13%
918 9%
1805
Fréchet-
Aure
Cierp-Gaud
Couledoux
Autrech

10
Gripp
Aspin-
Aure
Arreau
Jézeau
6
Cazaux-
Layrisse
Burgalays
Baren
Gouaux-de-Luchon
N125
Fos
Saint-Béat
Caneján
Bordius

Mongie
l'Arbizon
2831
Cadéac
Lançon
Ancizan
Bordères-
Louron
Bourg-
d'Oueil
Sommet
d'Antenac
1990
Mayrègne
D125
Bausen
Lès
Montauban-
de-Luchon
9%
Arres
Vilamòs
Montlude
Bòssost • 2517
Vielha
Riu Varrados
Vall
d'Aran

Aulon
Gouaux
618
Saccourvielle
Cazeaux-
10%-de-Luchon
N230
Vila
Aubèrt
Vilac

Lac de l'Oule
Vielle-
Aure
Bourisp
Mont
Vielle-Louron
Louderville
Bagnères-
de-Luchon
Vielha

Tramezaigues
D929
St.-Lary-
Soulan
9%
Oô
Peyragudes
XII-IV
Benòs
Es Bordes
Betrèn

Aragnouet
D173
Loudenvielle
les Granges
d'Astau
Pic de Cécire
2403
Hospice
de Fran
46
2463
47
Gard

Pic d'Aret
2939
2803
141
Pic Schrader
3177
2321
43 44
45
48
Maladeta
• 3308
49
Vallibierna
3010
N230
126
3014

2889
39
Posets
3371
41
42
2840
E. Tort
de Rius

Punta Suelza
2974
N138
38
40
Benasque
Led

Bielsa
35
Gistaín
Serveto
Eriste
Sahún
139
Cerler
Pico de Vallibierna
3062
Vall de

2317
Salinas de Sín
Sín
San Juan de Plan
2628
10
2855
Les Caldes
de Boí
Senet

29
Tella
Lafortunada
Sarav
Plan
Sesué
Ramastué
Liri
Gallinero
2728
50
Bono
2420
Barrabés
Erill-La-Val

37
36
Villanova
Chía
Urmella
Castejón de Sos
Bisaurri
Denúy
Castanesa
Fonchanina
Viñal
2452
Barruera
Cardet
Du

2246
Cotiella
2912
Barbaruéns
Seira
Gabás
S.Feliú
de Veri
Llagunas
Ardanúy
Vilaller
Emb. de Llesp

Peña Montañesa
2291
San Lorién
Monasterio
de S. Victorián
Viu
Gabás
S.Martín de Veri
2115
Abella
Laspaúles
260
9%
Castarné
Montanuy
Llesp
Sarroqueta
Castelló de Tor
Malpàs

Los Molinos
El Pueyo
de Araguás
Fosado
Samper
Senz
Liert
Espès
El Turbón
2492
Vilas
del Turbón
1765
Bonansa
Calvera
Pont
de Suert
Viu
de Lle

Valle
Usana
260
Arro
Charo
Gerbe
Fuendecampo
Campo
Foradada
de Toscar
Rañín
Campanué
Navarri
Espluga
Torre la Ribera
Egea
Ballabriga
Beranúy
Pardinella
Santorens
1701 15

E. de
Fueva
Mediano
Tierrantona
El Humo
de Muro
Solipueyo 1550
Bacamorta
Morillo de Monclús
Formigales
Santa Liestra
y San Quílez
Villacarli
Merli
1550
Soperún
Serraduy
Pallerol
El Sas
Sopeira
1490
25 de Sant

N138
1178
Palo
Samitier
Troncedo
Centenera
Esdolomada
Roda
La Puebla
de Roda
Rivera del Vall

1 Ibón de Anayet, 2225m

A peat lake in wonderful mountain surroundings

Corral de las Mulas – Ibón de Anayet and back

Location: Sallent de Gállego, 1305m.
Starting point: Corral de las Mulas, 1600m, on the road to the Col du Portalet. A good 2km beyond the exit to Formigal, the approach to the Anayet lift area is signposted to the left. The road is usually closed off outside the ski season so that you have to park at the buildings near the road.
Walking times: Corral de las Mulas – Ibón

de Anayet 2¼ hrs.; return 1¾ hrs.; total time 4 hrs.
Difference in height: 625 m.
Grade: red and white marked GR path. The short final ascent to the plateau with the lakes is a bit steeper.
Recommended map: Valle de Tena, 1:40.000; publ. by Editorial Pirineo 1997.
Stops and accommodation: bars and restaurants in Sallent de Gállego.

The ascent through the valley of the Barranco de Culibillas leads through a charming landscape of streams onto a vast high plateau crossed by soft rolling grass-covered hills and holding the Ibón de Anayet. In the west and in the south it is enclosed by a moderately high mountain chain where the steep flanked Pico de Anayet rises in competition with the Pic du Midi d'Ossau towering up in the background on the French side. Both mountains are mainly of volcanic origin.

From the **Corral de las Mulas** walk about 3km on the surfaced track to Anayet lift station. A track continues beyond the lift area which you follow as far as the first left-hand bend with a large cairn. Take the path branching off right here and after a few minutes you come to a signpost for the Ibones de Anayet. Your path goes beside the stream along the sloping banks, then

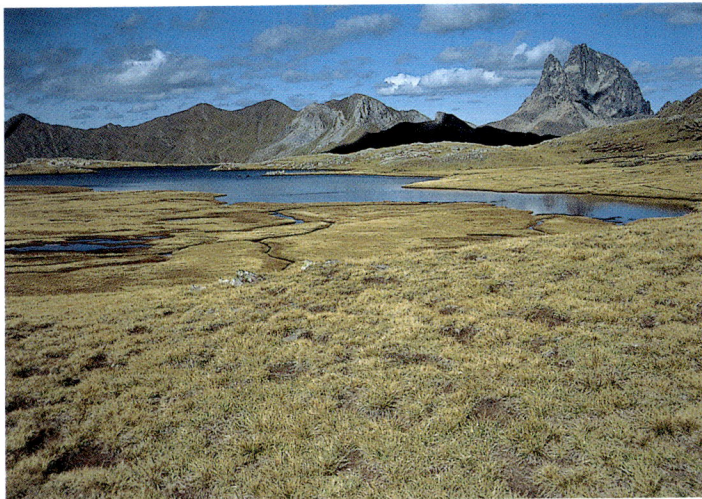

Ibón de Anayet and Pic du Midi d'Ossau.

swings to the west and leads into the broad valley of the Barranco de Culibillas. After a comfortable ascent you come to a small plain and afterwards the valley gets steep again and you change over onto the right-hand bank of the stream. The path here heads for a conspicuous hill with a jagged ridge which you go round to the right. Where the valley levels out again, change over to the other side of the stream once more. The broad ascending hillside is clearly visible ahead and the high plateau with the lakes extends beyond. The path leads you up a gradual incline through large reddish boulders and then, after crossing the stream again, a substantial uphill climb begins round quite long bends up to the wide and hilly plateau bordered by a long wall of rocks with the Pico de Anayet in the north. The path heads towards the Pico and reaches the shallow **Ibón de Anayet**, 2225m, which you can easily walk around close to the water's edge.

If you continue along the GR path on the left of the lake in a northerly direction you will come to the edge of the plateau and there you can zigzag down to the point where the impressive waterfall cascades down at the head of the Canal Royal valley, called La Rinconada. From here you can enjoy a magnificent view down into the valley.

2 To the Embalse de Escarra and through the gorge of the Barranco de Escarrilla

Exciting round walk through varied landscapes

Escarrilla – Salto del Río Escarra – Collado de la Cochata – Punta Cochata – Camino de los Forzados – Escarrilla

Location: Escarrilla, 1185m.

Starting point: old road just before the Escarrilla tunnel, 1210m. The old road from Escarrilla in the direction of Sallent de Gállego turns off right, directly before the tunnel entrance (only open to hikers and cyclists) and you park here. If there are no parking spaces, park on the other side of the road in a larger lay-by.

Walking times: car park – Salto del Río Escarra 1¼ hrs.; Salto del Río Escarrilla – Collado de la Cochata 1¼ hrs.; Collado de la Cochata – Punta Cochata ½ hrs.; Punta Cochata – Camino de las Forzados 1¼ hrs.; Camino de las Forzados – Escarrilla 1¾ hrs.; total time 6 hrs. (Without the ascent to Punta Cochata, a good 5 hours.)

Difference in height: 690m.

Grade: strenuous walk predominantly on yellow and white marked PR paths; path to Collado de la Cochata sparingly marked with red and white, but without any route-finding problems. The ascent to Punta Cochata is very steep and demands sure-footedness on short scrambling sections (I). Much of the walk is in the shade but it can be very hot in summer.

Recommended map: Panticosa-Formigal, 1:25.000; published by Editorial Alpina 2001

Stops and accommodation: bars und restaurants in Escarrilla.

Tip: the round walk is still worthwhile even if you leave out the detour to the Salto del Río Escarrilla and / or the ascent up to Punta Cochata.
Possibility of a link with with Walk 3.

This round walk provides you with a wealth of contrasting impressions. It begins with a walk to the large cascade at the deep cleft at the exit from the gorge of Garganta del Río Escarra and continues with a gentle climb up to the Collado de la Cochata beyond which are situated the extensive green pastured slopes in front of the fabulous mountain backdrop of the Sierra de la Partacua. It then makes an intermediary detour onto the Punta Cochata, whose steep ascent is rewarded with a magnificent panorama, and eventually leads along the Camino de los Forzados, high up in the rocks of the gorge, through wonderful forests back into the valley.

From the **car park** go across the Río Escarra on the bridge for a few metres back to the track which branches off right from the road. A signpost for El Saldo points towards the first objective of the walk. After a few paces the track divides and you continue uphill to the left and take the hiking trail which immediately bears left again. This soon meets a track, continues on the other side of it and then forks after a few paces. Keep right and afterwards the path crosses two streams, one after the other, very quickly starts to ascend and then gradually leaves the dense mixed forest. Mostly enclosed by tall box trees it runs across sloping meadows to a track where

El saldo: impressive exit from the Barranco de Escarrilla.

you continue to the right and reach some livestock fencing. (Close the gate again behind you) The track soon becomes an old roadway which goes gently downhill. After a few minutes you branch off to the left (there's wooden post with waymarkings) and cross the meadows. As the striking silhouette of Punta Cochata rises in the west you head towards the fantastic rock formations of the Escarra gorge. The path leads through rocky ground with metre-high box trees, it is then reinforced shortly before the exit to the gorge and descends to the round pool at the foot of the **Salto del Río Escarra**, 1440m. If the level of the water is not too high you can easily cross over boulders onto the other side of the stream from where you can see the narrow and twisting rock cleft head-on. To continue the round walk you first have to return along the path to the livestock fencing, and just before it, take the old roadway which bears off right from the track and is marked red and white further on. Climb up across sloping pastures in the direction of Punta Cochata and after 20minutes you cross a stream and the roadway gets narrower after that. As soon as it starts to descend, leave it to the left along an ascending grassy path (cairn), which heads across the sloping meadows towards the broad col in the south of the sheer Punta Cochata. On the right of the path there's a sea of enormous boulders under which a village lies buried, according to legend.

When you have reached the flat and broad **Collado de la Cochata**, 1775m, walk across to the slope leading down from the col in the west. Do not descend there. Walk along beside the foothills of Punta Cochata for a little while longer to the north-west until you are standing below the wide break in the band of rock. Heading towards this, climb up the steep slope to the bottom of the rocks where a small section of climbing awaits you, but with good footholds and handholds. After that some occasional cairns lead you through steep grassy and rocky terrain (keeping more to the right at first, then a little more to the left further up) quickly up to **Punta Cochata**, 1900m, where you can enjoy a fantastic view from the long and narrow ridge. Back at the starting point for the ascent follow the path across the western slope of Punta Cochata which soon turns off in the direction of the reservoir, descends across the slope to the bank and then leads on the right to a house ruin. Behind this, walk over the dam to the other side of the lake, continue there along the easily ascending path across the slope above Río Escarra. Keep to the right at a junction and reach a crossroads with signposts and take the path to Escarilla (you can link this walk with Walk 3 along the marked path to the Collado de Pazino). It is now waymarked with yellow and white again and runs at first gently uphill across the slopes covered in box trees, gorse and bushes towards the cleft of the gorge. At another fork after walking for a while through a wood you come to the start of the **Camino de los Forzados** ('path of the convict labourers'), 1560m, which was laid by political prisoners under the reign of Franco for the purpose of transporting materials to build the dam. Straight ahead goes to Sallen, but you follow the descending Camino to the right, which soon becomes narrow zigzags which have been cut into the rock. After the steep descent on the high rock face of the gorge with its striking colours and shapes, there follow some lengthy sloping bends which run through a beautiful mixed forest. The path then joins an old roadway and you meet a track which you follow to the right. This brings you to the old road. Go right here and after 100m come back to the starting point.

Punta Cochata.

3 Punta del Pacino, 1970m

Inconspicuous summit with wonderful views into the distance

Sallent de Gállego – Collado del Pacino – Punta del Pacino and back

Location: Sallent de Gállego, 1325m.
Starting point: on the road from Sallent de Gállego to Formigal (A-136), about 200m beyond the exit to Sallent, there's a track branching off left at a green water pipe, 1360m. PR signpost for Collado del Pacino.
Walking times: starting point – Collado del Pacino 1¼ hrs., Collado del Pacino – Punta del Pacino ½ hr.; return 1¼ hrs.; total time 3 hrs.

Difference in height: 610m
Grade: easy walk along yellow and white marked PR path as far at the Collado del Pacino. Summit ascent to a large extent without paths, but marked with cairns.
Recommended map: Panticosa-Formigal, 1:25,000; published by Editorial Alpina 2001.
Stops and accommodation: bars and restaurants in Sallent de Gállego.
Possibility of combining: with Walk 2.

At first glimpse Punta del Pacino seems anything other than an attractive objective, but its strategic position makes this unimposing peak a first-class viewpoint from where you can look across the important mountain chains of the Valle de Tena.

View of the Sierra Partacua.

Barranco de Escarrilla.

First follow the gently inclined **forest track** for a good kilometre, keep left at the next two forks and then it becomes old tracks which lead you into a beech wood. Here you meet a broad path which ascends gently up round some bends, passes through a cattle gate (close it behind you) and leaves the forest again. Now walk over carpets of grass past a water tower on your left to which there's a short detour: from here onwards you can enjoy open views of some noteworthy peaks in the northern Valle de Tena – Peña Foratata, Picos de Musales, Garmo Negro, Infierno, Argualas.

Back on the path continue to climb up the slope round wide bends, come again through a small birch wood and after several bends on the open slope you reach the **Collado del Pacino**, 1830m. Behind the ridge of the col begins a well-trodden path which leads to the east. Follow this and after a short while start the summit ascent on grassy scars and small-stoned scree. The path loses itself from time to time on the eroded slope, but the numerous cairns always lead you back to the correct path.

Without any difficulty you reach the **Punta del Pacino**, 1970m, with the trig point.

4   Ibones de Arriel, 2260m

Clear mountain lakes in majestic surroundings

La Sarra – Plano Cheto – Ibón de Arriel Bajo – Ibón de Arriel Alto and back

Location: Sallent de Gállego, 1305m.
Starting point: car park at the end of the Embalse de La Sarra, 1445m. From Sallent de Gállego a road leads to the reservoir (signposted 'La Sarra'), go along here past the electricity works to the car park.
Walking times: La Sarra – Plano Cheto 1¼ hrs.; Plano Cheto – Ibón de Arriel Bajo 1½ hrs.; Ibón de Arriel Bajo – Ibón de Arriel Alto ½ hr.; return 2½ hrs.; total time 5¾ hrs.
Difference in height: 815m.
Grade: untaxing GR path as far as the Plano Cheto (marked red and white), a steep ascent up the slope after that – 150 vertical metres up an arduous scree slope. It's a leisurely path again between the lakes. From the fork there are red waymarkings and cairns. Shady as far as Plano Cheto, the steep ascent goes across open ground.
Recommended map: Panticosa-Formigal, 1:25,000; published by Editorial Alpina 2001.
Stops and accommodation: bar at the Embalse de La Sarra (only in summer); bars or restaurants in Sallent de Gállego.
Linking tip: can be combined with Walk 5.

The Ibones de Arriel are justifiably some of the most beautiful lake landscapes in the Pyrenees. The four lakes, lying on different plains, are surrounded by magnificently formed granite mountains and steep peaks, amongst which Pico Palas indisputably takes pride of place. At Ibón de Arriel Alto, the largest and most beautiful of the lakes, this truly majestic mountain stands directly in front of you.

At the end of the **Embalse de La Sarra** cross over the Río Aguas Limpias. The broad hiking trail begins immediately after the bridge (signpost for Refugio de Respomuso), which runs gently up and down through the once cultivated river valley. The gradient increases before a stream cascading down from the left. Cross this and the stream immediately following over a little concrete bridge. After that the path levels out again and enters a pretty beech wood.

Now walk close to the deep gorge which now and then allows you views of some beautiful cascades. The gentle path uphill becomes a little more strenuous for short periods and then you come to the confluence of the Barranco de Soba with the Río Aguas Limpias which, at this point, displays itself in a marvellous cascade at the exit to the narrow gorge (Paso del Onso).

Cross the Barranco de Soba running from the left over the concrete bridge and ignore soon afterwards the path branching off left which leads to the Collado de la Soba. Continue instead along the edge of the gorge and then,

Majestic surroundings of the Ibones de Arriel.

Ibón de Arriel Bajo.

as it runs on the level, the path moves closer to the river. The valley broadens out and you come out into the idyllic valley plain of **Plano Cheto**, 1680m, with small meadows and a delightful beech wood. Further ahead you can see the big cascade of the Barranco de Arriel. The path heads towards this which you go across on the boulders (be careful if the water level is high), and then the path begins to get quite a bit steeper.

At the following fork leave the GR to the left, and go straight on to the Refugio de Respomuso (see Walk 5) and ascend the steep slope.

After you have negotiated the first steep part, the path levels out noticeably, comes closer to the Barranco de Arriel, runs along the right-hand bank for a while and then changes over at a cairn onto the other side.

The strenuous climb up the scree slope round the huge rockslide of the waterfall begins here. After you have climbed 150 vertical metres the path swings slowly to the east and becomes a more gentle incline up the slope which leads to the Barranco de Arriel.

Walk beside the cleft of the gorge across the left-hand scree slope to reach a reservoir. At the end of this you can see a reinforced path running back on the right on the slope which leads, approximately at the same height, over to the Refugio de Respomuso (there's a good opportunity here to link with Walk 5).

Ibón de Arriel Alto and Pico Palas.

The path now runs through the corridor of rock on the left-hand bank and afterwards you come to the **Ibón de Arriel Bajo**, 2180m, which you walk along on the right-hand side. At the end of the lake cross over the stream again and head towards the rise in the rocks where you can see the dam of the higher lake. A turn-off left marked with a cairn goes up to the dam and continues to the left hand bank of the lake, but you stay for the time being on the broad stabilised path going straight on. Walk at the foot of the rock slope and then after a sharp bend in the path head towards an overflow wall. Just before that, a fairly indistinct grassy path turns off right (look out for the cairn) which ascends the granite hump. Once at the top you are standing a few metres above the wonderfully situated **Ibón de Arriel Alto**, 2260m, and can start looking for the best place on the gently undulating terrain to enjoy a well-earned view.

5 Refugio de Respomuso (Circo de Piedrafita), 2200m

Through the Río Aguas Limpias valley to a huge circle of mountains

La Sarra – Refugio de Respomuso and back

Location: Sallent de Gállego, 1305m.
Starting point: car park at the end of the Embalse de La Sarra, 1445m. A road goes from Sallent de Gállego to the reservoir (signpost for La Sarra), past the electricity works there as far as the car park.
Walking times: La Sarra – Refugio de Respomuso 3 hrs.; return 2½ hrs.; total time 5½ hrs.
Difference in height: 755m.
Grade: altogether a very strenuous walk on well-made GR path (marked red and white).
Recommended map: Sallent de Gállego, 1:25,000, Mapa Topográfico Nacional de España; published by Instituto Geográfico Nacional, 2000.
Stops and accommodation: bar at the Embalse de La Sarra (only in summer); the Refugio de Respomuso is staffed all year round, be sure to book accommodation and food by telephone: ℂ 974 490203.
Linking Tip: with Walk 4.

The Balaitús massif in the north and the row of peaks around Gran Facha in the east are the defining elements of the Circo de Piedrafita which was once encompassed by a large glacier. Today the numerous water courses are

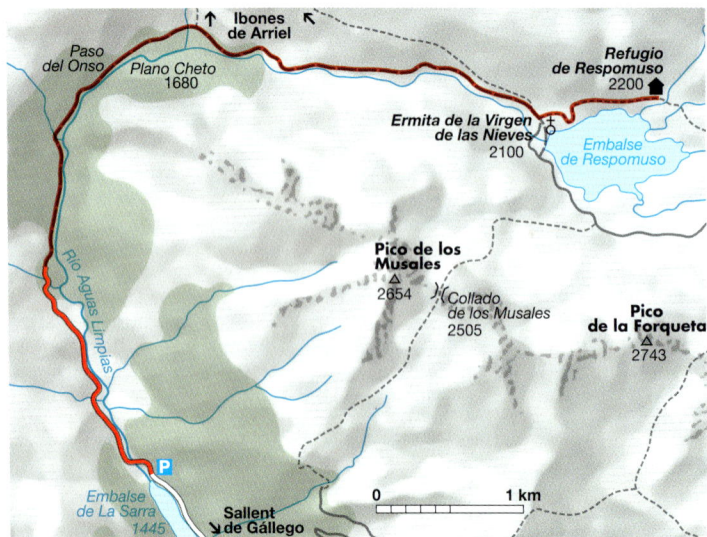

Circo de Piedrafita with the Refugio de Respomuso on the left.

dammed up in the Embalse de Respomuso on whose bank lies the hut of the same name. It is the central starting point for classic mountain routes and multi-day walks which is why the *refugio* is often used in summer.

The first part of the walk is identical with Walk 4. At the signposted fork to the Ibones de Arriel continue straight ahead along the red and white marked GR path on the left bank of the Río Aguas Limpias. The steep gradient continues steadily, forced in between times through small ledges and only slackens off when you reach the height of the Embalse de Respomuso. Shortly before the dam the path branches off to the left (a large cairn), then leaves the Ermita Virgen de las Nieves, 2100m, towering up at the end of the dam on your right-hand side, passes a signpost for Respomuso and soon begins to wind up the slope which brings you to the height of the mountain hut lying further ahead on a plateau on the slope above the lake. (On the way a path joins from the left which comes over from the Ibón de Arriel Bajo, possible to link here with Walk 4). Then the path maintains height across the slopes to a fork where it branches off right to the **Refugio de Respomuso**, 2200m.

6 Ibones Azules, 2410m

To the 'blue lakes' at the foot of the Picos de l'Infierno

Balneario de Panticosa – Ibones de Bachimaña – Ibones Azules and back

Location: Balneario de Panticosa, 1635m.
Starting point: main square in Balneario de Panticosa. In summer you have to park before the village.
Walking times: Balneario – Ibones de Bachimaña 1¾ hrs.; Ibones de Bachimaña – Ibón Azul Alto 1¼ hrs., return 2½ hrs.; total time 5½ hrs.
Difference in height: 775m.
Grade: not a difficult walk along well-made GR path (marked red and white). Steep gradient as far as the Mirador de la Reina and on the ascent to the Ibones de Bachimaña, otherwise comfortable incline.
Recommended map: Sallent de Gállego, 1:25,000, Mapa Topográfico Nacional de España; published by Instituto Geográfico Nacional, 2000.
Stops and accommodation: bars and restaurants in Balneario de Panticosa.
Linking Tip: with Walk 7.

The mountain regions of the Valle de Tena are full of small and larger lakes, almost all of them relics of the last ice age. A considerable number of them

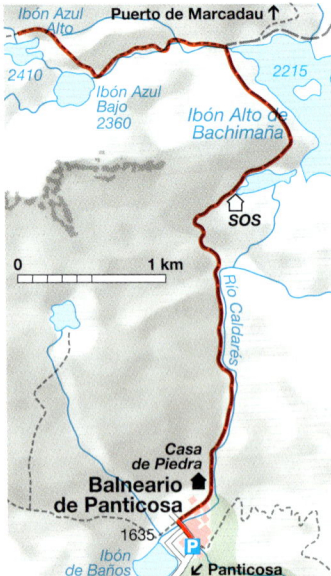

lie in the mountain valleys above Balneario de Panticosa, amongst them the famous and much-visited Ibones Azules, dominated by the three peaks of Picos de l'Infierno and all of them just above the three thousand metre boundary. A well-made bridle path leads to the lakes which was laid for the purpose of building the dam at the Ibón Alto de Bachimaña and it runs through the enchanting valley of Río Caldares.

At the **Plaza Mayor** in Balneario de Panticosa keep left along the road through the village, go past Hotel Continental, then head to the right out of the village. The road ends at the electricity works and on the bend before this, the hiking trail branches off to the Ibones Azules. Straight away it ascends quickly and soon rises above the village. After a steep 20 minute climb you come past the Mirador de la Reina, then the path runs through granite boulders and comes close to the Barranco de Caldares. Along the way you catch many glimpses of the pretty cascades and pools. A short ascent through a rock corridor leads temporarily away from the stream. After that you come closer to the stream again and reach a small viewpoint overlooking a beautiful waterfall. The path now goes round a bend and levels out visibly while the stream runs gently over rock steps and projections. The broader valley lies ahead with pretty grassy slopes and islands of rock. At a fork in the path continue along the left bank of the Río Caldares, walk through a delightful landscape of streams and then head towards the abrupt head of the valley above which lie the Ibones de Bachimaña. The path avoids the steep rock face and

Picos de l'Infierno.

bends to the left onto the less precipitous western slope and there winds round numerous bends uphill and crosses over to the small lake at the foot of the huge overflow wall. (On the opposite side of the lake there's a *refugio* with an emergency telephone.) A short climb on the left bank brings you to the large **Ibón Alto de Bachimaña**, 2215m. The good stabilised path now runs above the lake, mostly on the level, across the sloping bank which is covered in boulders, and only at the end descends to the stream which then runs into the reservoir. Cross the inflowing stream and smaller side streams over some stones. Immediately after that you come to a fork at a large cairn where the path branches off right to the Puerto de Marcadau (possibility of linking with Walk 7; signpost for Bramatuero), but keep straight ahead, on the right of the stream, climb up the slope with the widely fanned cascade ahead and reach the **Ibón Azul Bajo**, 2360m, at the foot of the Oicos l'Infierno (the tin bivouac hut on the bank of the lake only serves as an emergency shelter). The path continues on the right-hand side of the lake and climbs the slope up to the 50m higher **Ibón Azul Alto**, 2410m.

7 Puerto de Marcadau, 2545m, and Pico de la Muga, 2675m

First class panoramic path to the pass into the French Marcadau valley

Balneario de Panticosa – Ibon Alto de Bachimaña – Puerto de Marcadau – Pico de la Muga and back

Location: Balneario de Panticosa, 1635m.
Starting point: Balneario de Panticosa. In the summer you must park outside the village.
Walking times: Balneario – Ibon Alto de Bachimaña 1¾ hrs.; Ibon Alto de Bachimaña – Puerto de Marcadau 1¾ hrs., Puerto de Marcadau – Pico de la Muga ½ hrs.; return 3¼ hrs.; total time 7¼ hrs.
Difference in height: 910m as far as Puerto de Marcadau; 1040m to Pico de la Muga.
Grade: long and altogether strenuous walk; on well-made GR path as far as the Ibón Alto de Bachimaña, marked red and white; after that on clear hiking trail with sections of steep climbing; cairns.

Recommended map: Sallent de Gállego, 1:25,000, Mapa Topográfico Nacional de España; published by Instituto Geográfico Nacional, 2000.
Stops and accommodation: bars and restaurants in Balneario de Panticosa.
Alternative: Circo de Pecico, 2560m: from the steep Arista de Pecico enclosed mountain basin south of Gran Facha. At the fork below Puerto de Marcadau take the narrow path to the left which runs along beside the small lake to the Ibón Grande de Pecico reservoir, 2465m. Cross the stream there, walk left along the south bank and then climb in a westerly direction up to the tiny Ibones Superiores de Pecico, 2560m. There and back takes 1¾ hrs. from the fork.

In comparison to the Ibones Azules nearby only a few people make the trek to the Puerto de Marcadau. This varied path has a load of splendid views to offer, amongst them the famous Gran Facha with its neighbouring peaks, the Batanes mountains and the granite basin eroded by glaciers with its lake-filled hollows. The view into the Marcadau valley from the pass on the border is rather disappointing because the Pico de la Muga blocks the view, but you can easily make up for this by climbing the peak, just over 100m higher, with a much more open view of the valley.

Follow Walk 6 as far as the fork in the paths beyond the **Ibón Alto de Bachimaña**. When you arrive there, continue along the path signposted to Bramatuero to the right. It begins to go uphill immediately and crosses the rocky slope which inclines down to the lake. The path then descends a little and continues above the lake. Keep left uphill at the next fork (the path going down to the valley floor leads over to the granite slopes beyond which the Embalse de Bramatuero Bajo is situated).

During a longer section the path cuts the slope and flat sections alternate with steeper ones, then you meet another fork where you again stay on the left path going uphill and walk over terrain with strikingly red-coloured rock. After another longer incline across the slope, follow some short loops in the path which bring you to a small platform on the slope with meadows and pools. Walk through the enchanting landscape with a wide view to the south-east across the lakes and the mountain chain surrounding them.

A short up-and-down section of the path brings you closer to the

On the way to the Puerto de Marcadau.

Barranco de la Canal coming down from the lakes of the Circo de Pecico. Cross the stream and go along beside it on the right as far as the long and small Ibón de Pecico where the path ascends the right bank (on the way ignore the narrow path [see Alternative] turning off left). After the path turns away from the lake it begins ascending the slope to the col and after a few long hairpin bends, reaches the **Puerto de Marcadau**, 2545m. From here ascend in a north-easterly direction along the broad ragged mountain ridge without any difficulties up to the **Pico de la Muga**, 2675m, where you are rewarded with a truly fabulous view.

8   On the Camino de Brazato

A narrow bridle path with the most beautiful views

Balneario de Panticosa – Embalse de Brazato and back

Location: Balneario de Panticosa, 1635m.
Starting point: Balneario de Panticosa. In summer you have to park outside the village.
Walking times: Balneario – Embalse de Brazato 2¼ hrs.; return 1¾ hrs.; total time 4 hrs.
Difference in height: 735 m.
Grade: easy walk on stabilised GR path (marked red and white).
Recommended map: Sallent de Gállego, 1:25,000, Mapa Topográfico Nacional de España; published by Instituto Geográfico Nacional, 2000.
Stops and accommodation: bars and restaurants in Balneario de Panticosa.
Alternative: Ibones Altos de Brazato (short, but really steep ascent): at the Embalse de Brazato stay on the path along the left bank. It runs on the level at first, then ascends and turns away from the

lake and climb up the steep slope round narrow bends, always on the left of the stream which flows from the lakes. Cairns mark the route and the path levels out over to the plateau on the slope and runs through rocky hills to the largest of the Ibones Altos de Brazato, 2460m, with a magnificent view of the Picos Garmo Negro, Argualas and Infierno on the western side of the Panticosa valley and the Sierra Partacua in the background. There and back 1 hr. **Puerto de Brazato:** continuation from the Ibones Altos de Brazato onto the pass to the Ara valley with a view of the Vignemale massif. The path continues on the right of the two large lakes at the foot of the Pico Baciás; it runs up a moderate incline across the slope to the gently sweeping Collado de Brazato, 2575m. There and back from Ibones Altos de Brazato, 1hr.

The old bridle path up to the Embalse de Brazato was once used for the building of the dam and is used today as a popular hiking trail. Even if the lake itself is framed by a rather unspectacular circle of mountains, the extensive views of the magnificent mountain backdrop and the diversity in the surrounding landscape, guarantee an impressive experience walking along effortless paths.

At the **Plaza Mayor** of Balneario de Panticosa ascend the broad steps on the right leading up to the sacred well. At a wooden sign with various directional information, amongst which you will also see a sign for the Ibones de Brazat', continue left, cross the canalised streambed and set off along the comfortable path. Leave it to the left after a few bends (many waymarkers), come past a large avalanche barrier and after that you arrive at a junction: on the left there's an alternative

The mighty backdrop of the three-thousanders dominates the Ibones de Brazato.

path signposted to the 'Ibones Azules, but your objective lies to the right. From now on the path ascends up the slope round wide bends through pine trees, juniper and rhododendrons and crosses a large sea of granite boulders in between. While you can enjoy a marvellous view of the noteworthy row of peaks on the other side of the valley, the Sierra Partacua comes into view in the background. At a fork with red waymarkings on a rock (left to 'Labaza') continue along the path to the right and make a long crossing over towards a conspicuous ridge on the slope coming down from the left in between times across an open scree slope. On a gentle grassy path ascend the open ridge, then the path becomes stony again, levels out and comes to a large water pipe. Here there's another junction where you keep left according to the waymarkers, cross over the water pipe and then go through a confusion of boulders with cairns to help you find the way. Then ascend the northern granite slope round brief bends (shortcuts over the scree are not worth the effort and the easier path is indicated with waymarkers and cairns), and after a long diagonal path reach the **Embalse de Brazato**, 2370m, dammed up in a narrow mountain basin.

9   Lake walk in the Valle Sabocos

Unusual round walk at the foot of the Peña Sabocos

Sabocos lift station – Ibón de Sabocos – Collado de Sabocos – Ibón de los Asnos –Sabocos lift station

Location: Panticosa, 1185m.
Starting point: chair-lift mountain station at the Ibón de Sabocos, 1940m.
Walking times: mountain station – Collado de Sabocos ¾ hr., Collado de Sabocos – Ibón de los Asnos 1 hr., Ibón de los Asnos – mountain station ¼ hr.; total time 2 hrs.
Difference in height: 180m.
Grade: easy PR path (marked yellow and white) as far as the Collado de Sabocos; from there as afar as the Ibón de los Asnos prediminantly without paths over some-times precipitous terrain; cairns only now and then. Some route-finding ability and sure-footedness required.
Recommended map: Valle de Tena, 1:40,000; published by Editorial Pirineo, 1997.
Stops and accommodation: bars and restaurants in Panticosa; restaurant at the mountain station of the chair-lift (open from 13.00 to 16.00).
Alternatives: Punta del Verde, 2295m: very beautiful viewpoint over the Collado de Sabocos. From the Collado you climb the at first broad, south ridge of Punta. At the steep summit section do not head directly for the summit, but continue the ascent in a northerly direction on the less steep side of the slope and then turn left to the summit. There and back 1 ¼ hrs.
Rincón del Verde, 1900m: the small valley pasture east of Collado de Sabocos lies in the shade of the fantastically struc-tured Tendeñera flanks. At the Collado keep on the yellow and white marked path which heads across softly undulating slopes straight for the green valley basin with the hut. There and back 2 hrs.
Pico Mandilar, 2220m: a first class viewing hilltop with far-reaching view across the Valle de Tena. At the western side of the Ibón de los Asnos take the path to the Collado de Bazuelo and climb the southern slope of Mandilar from there up to Pico. There and back from Ibón de los Asnos 1½ hrs.
Tip: cable car and chair-lift from Panticosa to the Ibón de Sabocos are in operation between 30th June and 9th September daily from 10.00; last cable car 18.15 (as of 2001). Up-to-date information from the Tourist Information in Panticosa.

Ibón de Sabocos.

The ski lifts of Panticosa bring many visitors in summer up into the Valle de Sabocos at the edge of the bizarre backdrop of rocks of the Sierra de Tendeñera. While most visitors are content with a short expedition to the two lakes remaining in glacier basins at the foot of the Peñas Sabocos and Roya, you can walk along isolated paths where the contrast is especially impressive between soft

grassy hills and precipitous, dramatic mountain formations. You can vary this relatively short walk with several worthwhile secondary objectives and it can be extended to make an extremely varied day trip.

At the **mountain station** for the chair-lift follow the signpost for Valle de los Saboco. After only a few minutes you reach a small elevation from where the yellow and white marked path quickly descends to the **Ibón de Sabocos**, 1905m, which is dominated by the striking Peña Sabocos. After the hut by the lake, cross over the outflowing stream and ascend across the grass-covered slope with stones and boulders along beside a stream gully running down from the east. The beaten path with waymarkers and cairns keeps first on the left of the broad stream hollow, changes further up onto the other side and continues to ascend the grass-covered slope. After a short section along the rocky stream gully you come into a small grassy hollow where there's a signpost (Valle de la Ripera / Panticosa) and straight after that you are standing on the **Collado de Sabocos**, 2090m, with a magnificent view of the steep fissured rocks of the Sierra de Tendeñera. (From the Collado you can make a detour up to the Punta del Verde or down to the Rincón del Verde – see Alternatives). Continue the round walk along a path which is obvious at first, branching off from the Collado in a south-westerly direction, and heads towards the foothills of the Peña Sabocos. After a level stretch the path inclines steeply and becomes increasingly unclear so that you can easily lose your way. The path is also

In the Valle de Sabocos.

criss-crossed with animal tracks. Do not stay too low on the slope because otherwise the steep flanks and the sharp cleft of the *barranco* dropping down into the Ibón de Sabocos will stop you from going any further. There are few cairns along this section, so keep high enough up towards the *barranco* and cross over the flat streambed without any problems. On the other side, climb up a small rocky projection and immediately afterwards, now waymarked with numerous cairns, descend the steep slope again towards a second *barranco* (be especially careful on this section if the grass is wet). Cross this *barranco* too, scramble up the rocks for a while on the other side, then the path becomes clear again and continues easily uphill at the foot of a rock face and soon joins a track. Follow this and after a few minutes you reach the **Ibón de los Asnos**, 2060m, with the bizarrely formed Peña Roya as a backdrop. You can walk round the small lake on a narrow path. From its north side several paths and shortcuts lead quickly down to the mountain station of the chair-lift.

Ibón de los Asnos.

49

10 Through the Valle del Río Ara

Enchanting valley walk along the wild Río Ara

San Nicolás de Bujaruelo – Refugio de Ordiso – Refugio de Labaza – Barranco de Batanes and back

Location: Torla, 1030m.
Starting point: San Nicolás de Bujaruelo, 1340m, at the end of the track through the Valle de Bujaruelo. About a 30 minute drive along the track.
Walking times: San Nicholás – Refugio de Ordiso 1½ hrs., Refugio de Ordiso – Refugio de Labaza 1¼ hrs.; Refugio de Labaza – Barranco de Batanes 1½ hrs.; return 3¼ hrs.; total time 7½ hrs.

Difference in height: 680m.
Recommended map: Vignemale-Bujaruelo, 1:30,000; published by Editorial Alpina, 1999.
Grade: easy, but long walk on GR path, marked red and white; broad track as far as the Refugio de Ordiso, after that a clear path with a mostly pleasant incline.
Refreshments: bars or restaurants in Torla; bar in San Nicolás (only in summer).

Arched bridge at Bujaruelo.

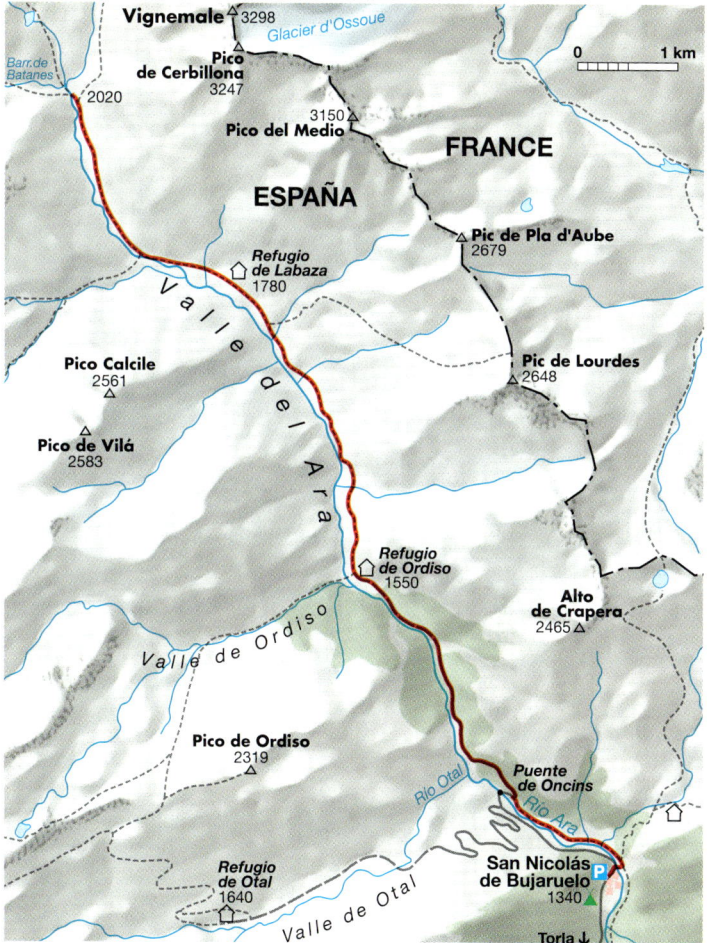

Vignemale 3298
Glacier d'Ossoue
Pico de Cerbillona 3247
Barr. de Batanes
2020
Pico del Medio 3150
FRANCE
ESPAÑA
Refugio de Labaza 1780
Pic de Pla d'Aube 2679
Valle del Ara
Pico Calcile 2561
Pic de Lourdes 2648
Pico de Vilá 2583
Refugio de Ordiso 1550
Valle de Ordiso
Alto de Crapera 2465
Pico de Ordiso 2319
Puente de Oncins
Río Otal
Río Ara
Refugio de Otal 1640
San Nicolás de Bujaruelo 1340
Valle de Otal
Torla ↓

0   1 km

The Río Ara reaches San Nicolás de Bujaruelo as an already considerably large mountain river. Before that it runs a long way through a wonderful valley where the diverse landscape varies from quiet pastures with meandering streams and a splendid array of flowers to the thundering depths of the gorge. This extremely enjoyable walk is not particularly strenuous and will reveal its diverse charms along the way. The walk, as it is described here, takes at least 7 hours.

In **San Nicolás de Bujaruelo** cross over the Río Ara on the medieval Puente de Bujaruelo and immediately afterwards, take the path branching off left (do not follow the uphill path to the Puerto de Bujaruelo!) which keeps to the Río Ara bank. (You can also walk along the roadway on the other river bank which begins before the bridge at a boulder with the waymarker for Otal on it.) It leads through the wonderful river valley and near the Puente de Oncins meets the roadway again which you follow to the right. After a sharp left-hand bend climb steeply up to one of the corridors cut out of the rock and then runs mostly on the level high above the river through the narrow gorge. On the way you pass a rock, lying on the left of the track, with the indistinct waymarker for Puente Colgante (about 50m after a sign for Coto de Pesca) and you can take a 10 minute detour here along the forest path turning off left to a breathtaking suspension bridge across a roaring river. Further along the track you cross the Barranco Salto de Pich, after which the valley narrows again. Pass an iron gate and the valley ahead becomes increasingly more open and you quickly arrive at the **Refugio de Ordiso**, 1550m. (Self-catering hut for 4-6 people). The track ends here and you continue the walk along the path ascending on the right of the Refugio across slopes covered with box trees. Climb round a boulder on the steep valley slope beyond which the path becomes flatter again. After crossing a stream the temporarily stabilised path runs high above the river through a narrow point and afterwards across the grass-covered slopes and through little pinewoods in the increasingly broader valley. Cross over several side streams, climb over some gently sloping hilltops and head for a broad grassy hollow with granite boulders strewn everywhere, past the **Refugio de Labaza**, 1780m (self-catering hut for 4-6 people). Further along the plain you pass the broad valley of the Barranco de Espelunz coming in from the left and up a gentle incline, go past a rain gauge tower positioned between the main stream and a side branch.

For the time being stay beside the little side stream, then the path runs nearer to the main stream and you come to the end of the walk, the **Barranco de Batanes**, 2020m, which joins the Río Ara here in a beautiful waterfall. At this point the GR path leaves the valley and leads westwards over into the Valle de Tena.

Valle del Río Ara.

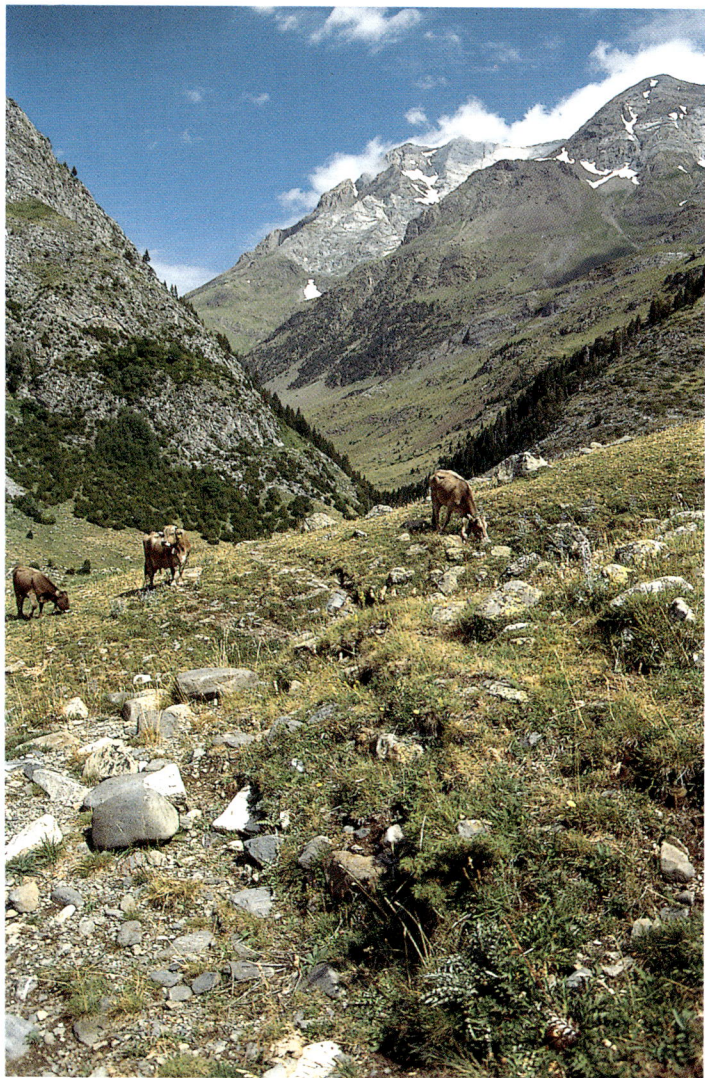

11 Valle de Otal

Idyllic high valley at the foot of the Tendeñera

San Nicolás de Bujaruelo – Refugio de Otal and back

Location: Torla, 1030m.
Starting point: San Nicolás de Bujaruelo, 1340m, at the end of the track through the Valle de Bujaruelo. About a 30 minute drive along the track.
Walking times: San Nicolás – Refugio de Otal 1¾ hrs., return 1¼ hrs.; total time 3 hrs.
Difference in height: 310m.
Grade: easy walking on track and GR path, marked red and white.
Recommended map: Vignemale-Bujaruelo, 1:30,000; published by Editorial Alpina, 1999.
Stops and accommodation: bars and restaurants in Torla; bar in San Nicolás (only in summer).
Alternative: Collado de Tendeñera, 2325m: attractive viewing point in the area around the Pico Tendeñera. 100m before the Refugio, the GR turns off right from the forest path at a large boulder (red and white waymarkings) to the Collado de Tendeñera. It runs at some distance past the hut and then ascends briskly up the right-hand slope to a plain situated higher up. Past a gauge for measuring rainfall the path continues up the slope, leads away from the stream and for a while down the valley. Then there's another climb up a slope after which you reach a cattle gate. Go past it on the left heading for a trig point. Be careful: about 50m beforehand, the path turns sharply to the right and runs past a boulder waymarked in red and white. After that it runs at a comfortable gradient, interrupted by some bends, across the slope down the valley. At a small stream it seems to continue straight ahead, but do not cross the stream, change direction instead beforehand and climb the hillside up the valley again to the long rock wall at the foot of which there's a narrow plateau. The path runs in a south-westerly direction to the clearly visible Collado de Tendeñera and goes up to the col. There and back from the Refugio de Otal, 4 hrs.

With its diversity of flowers, marshy meadows, mountain streams and colonies of marmots, the Valle de Otal presents an enchanting atmosphere and invites you to take a stroll along the winding Río Otal. The valley is cut off by the Circo de Otal where the towering Pico Tendeñera and the jagged

Valle de Otal.

massif of Peña Arañonera are located. The latter contains one of the largest cave systems in the Pyrennees. The walk can be extended if you climb up to the Collado de Tendeñera where you can enjoy a magnificent view of the Ara valley and the mountains around Bujaruelo.

In **San Nicolás de Bujaruelo** cross over the Río Ara on the medieval Puente de Bujaruelo and immediately afterwards take the path branching off left (do not follow the uphill path to the Puerto de Bujaruelo!) which keeps to the Río Ara bank. (You can also walk along the roadway on the other river bank which begins before the bridge at a boulder where the name of Otal is written.) It leads through the wonderful river valley and meets the roadway again near the Puente de Oncins. Right leads into the upper valley of the Rio Ara (see Walk 10), but you go left across the bridge as far as the junction and from there along the roadway which continues on the right up to the Valle de Otal round long hairpin bends. You can take several shortcuts along cross paths on the grassy slopes and then reach the threshold of the valley at a fence with a gate. Continue close to the stream and at a concrete crossing change over onto the other side of the Rio Otal which winds its way through the broad valley. Either walk without paths through the lush and sometimes marshy valley meadows to the head of the valley or continue to walk along the roadway which runs at the foot of the right-hand slopes through the flat valley to a point beyond the **Refugio de Otal**, 1640m, where it ends.

12 Ibón and Puerto de Bernatuara, 2335m

Isolated glacial lake and border pass with beautiful views

San Nicolás de Bujaruelo – Refugio de Sandaruelo – Ibón de Bernatuara – Puerto de Bernatuara and back

Location: Torla, 1030m.
Starting point: San Nicolás de Bujaruelo, 1340m, at the end of the track through the Valle de Bujaruelo. About a 30 minute drive along the track.
Walking times: San Nicolás – Refugio de Sandaruelo 1 hr.; Refugio de Sandaruelo – Ibón de Bernatuara 2 hrs.; Ibón de Bernatuara – Puerto de Bernatuara ½ hr.; return 2¾ hrs.; total time 6¼ hrs.
Difference in height: 995m.
Recommended map: Vignemale-Bujaruelo, to a scale of 1:30,000; published by Editorial Alpina, 1999.
Grade: altogether a very demanding walk because of the variation in height and the steep sections of ascent. A well-made path as far as the Barranco de Lapazosa; narrow paths further up, some of which are unclear. Waymarkers and cairns. Mostly without shade.
Stops and accommodation: bars and restaurants in Torla; bar in San Nicolás (only in summer).

The round Ibón de Bernatuara at the top of the pass between the Valle de Bujaruelo and the French Vallée de la Canau lies hidden in a rocky basin eroded by glaciers. The pass between Pic de Gabiet and Pico de la Bernatuara was formerly an important link for cattle herds which, still today, graze on the flower-covered slopes abundant with water. This walk, with its extremely diverse landscape, offers very beautiful views even on the ascent.
In **San Nicolás de Bujaruelo** change over onto the other side of the Río Ara on the Puente de Bujaruelo and follow the path to the Puerto de Bujaruelo (marked on a rock). The broad stony path immediately climbs steeply uphill and at the start winds up the wooded slope round short and then longer bends. The terrain increasingly thins out and you come close to a power line and walk parallel to it as far as a sign at an electricity mast warning you of avalanches. The path forks here: right continues to the Puerto de Bujaruelo (see Walk 13), but you turn off left (a yellow arrow and a sign for Ibón) and

find yourself getting closer to the Barranco de Lapazosa. The path goes along beside the deep gorge and quickly reaches the level of the wild stream. A yellow arrow indicates the best place to cross the streambed. On the opposite bank the path leads for a short while to the left, then changes direction and now climbs upstream again through a beech wood up to a sloping meadow. Follow the unclear tracks there, keep heading towards a pylon, then continue to a conspicuous solitary boulder on

Ibón de Bernatuara.

which you can see a cairn. On the right below lies the **Refugio de Sandaruelo**, 1680m, (the neglected hut is only usable as an emergency shelter). Once at the boulder a washed-out yellow arrow indicates the onward path to the Ibón. Ascend northwards across the sloping meadow and come to a smaller boulder with a yellow spot and another directional arrow, then the path becomes a well-trodden dirt path which quickly leads up to a grove of box trees then levels out beyond it and runs across the slopes of the Barranco Sandaruelo. A flat section brings you closer to a side stream which you cross over. First continue along the main stream until the path turns off to the west (cairn) and skirts a small elevation. Changing your direction to the north, climb up the hill and at the top the path gently descends to a small stream which you cross. The path loses itself a little in the marshy meadow. Traverse the meadow in a northerly direction and you soon join the well-trodden path again. After another stream crossing you come close to a very eroded slope which drops away from the foot of Pico de Bernatuara. Cairns in the gullies guide you up the best ascent route.

After this last stage of ascent the path runs through rock debris, goes round a small hilltop in a north-easterly direction and afterwards crosses over to the small col beyond which the almost circular lake lies in a deep hollow. A little way down the slope and you reach the **Ibón de Bernatuara**, 2270m. Continue there along the left bank to the hillside up to the pass lying opposite which you ascend at its left edge to the **Puerto de Bernatuara**, 2335m.

13 Puertos de Bujaruelo

Border crossings with views of the northern Marboré massif

San Nicolás de Bujaruelo – Puerto de Bujaruelo – Puerto Viejo de Bujaruelo – San Nicolás de Bujaruelo

Location: Torla, 1030m.
Starting point: San Nicolás de Bujaruelo, 1340m, at the end of the track through the Valle de Bujaruelo. About a 30 minute drive along the track.
Walking times: San Nicolás de Bujaruelo – Puerto de Bujaruelo 2½ hrs.; Puerto de Bujaruelo – Puerto Viejo de Bujaruelo 1¼ hrs.; Puerto Viejo de Bujaruelo – San Nicolás de Bujaruelo 2¼ hrs.; total time 6 hrs.
Difference in height: 1000m.
Grade: technically not very difficult, but because of the height difference and some steep sections it's a very strenuous walk on predominantly well-trodden paths; waymarkers and cairns. Be careful on the ascent to the Puerto de Bujaruelo where there can still be snow on the steep northern slopes even into early summer and a danger of avalanches!
Recommended map: Ordesa y Monte Perdido, 1:25,000 (Parques Nacionales de España 1); published by Ministerio de Fomento, 2000.
Stops and accommodation: bars and restaurant in Torla; bar in San Nicolás (only in summer).

The connecting pass between the Valle de Bujaruelo and the French Gavarnie is a first class viewpoint: as you look back you can see the whole of the Valle de Otal and the dramatic shape of Sierra de Tendeñera and in the south there's the huge backdrop of the Marboré peaks and their residual glaciers. The return across the Col de Tentes and two lakes, one on either side of the border, round off the walk.

In **San Nicolás de Bujaruelo** follow the path in Walk 12 as far as the fork. Go right here (red arrow on the rock) and ascend the steep grass-covered slopes on the well-trodden path. After you have quickly gained height the

path turns into scree-covered terrain and goes for a lengthy stretch across the slopes dropping away to the right. The easy ascent is interrupted by an intermediary steeper section across grassy slopes strewn with rocks and afterwards the cart track levels out again and heads for the Cabaña de 'Eléctricas' near to an electricity pylon. Walk along the Barranco de Lapazosa, pass the small hut (emergency shelter), come quickly

Sierra de Tendeñera.

to the level of the stream and cross over onto the other side. Walk along beside the stream on the left bank through the valley, Plana de Lacoma, past a side stream flowing in from the left down from the Ibón de Lapazosa. (This is the point where you join the path again on the return). After having crossed the stream continue uphill and head towards the clearly defined col. The path gets a bit steeper before a break in the slope and then changes over to the other side of the valley where it zigzags steeply up to the top of the pass.

At the **Puerto de Bujaruelo**, 2275m, go to the road which comes from Gavarnie and ends on the pass. Walk for just under 2km along this as far as the barrier and the car park. The massive mountain range between Gabieto and Marboré behind you becomes increasingly broader and more impressive as you look back. Leave the road at the car park to the left and follow the signposted path to the Lac des Espécières. At the lake walk along the right-hand bank and continue along the path to the pass which reaches the **Puerto Viejo de Bujaruelo**, 2340m, across some really steep grassy slopes. Go downhill from here to the Ibón de Lapazosa which you can walk round on the left or the right-hand side. At the end of the lake the path continues to descend between the outflow of the stream and the power line across grassy slopes, then crosses the stream, turns off to the south and follows the course of the stream down across the slopes till you join your original path. Go right here to return to San Nicolás de Bujaruelo.

Lac des Espécières.

14 Camino de Turieto

Quiet approach to the Valle de Ordesa

Torla – Pradera de Ordesa and back

Location: Torla, 1030m.
Starting point: Puente de la Glera, 970m. Just beyond Torla turn off right to the Río Ara campsite and drive to the bridge: either park here or continue for another good kilometre along the river as far as the signpost for Camino Turieto. You can also reach the bridge along a footpath from Torla.
Walking times: Puente de la Glera – Pradera de Ordesa 2¾ hrs; return 2¼ hrs.; total time 5 hrs.
Difference in height: 330m.

Grade: effortless walk on a well-made GR path (marked red and white).
Recommended map: Ordesa y Monte Perdido, 1:25,000 (Parques Nacionales de España 1); published by Ministerio de Fomento, 2000.
Stops and accommodation: restaurants in Torla; bar in the Pradera de Ordesa (only in summer).
Tip: if you want to avoid walking back, you can also return by bus to Torla in the summer (see section on 'Getting there').

The old path from Torla to the Pradera de Ordesa provides an ideal opportunity to make your first approach into the famous canyon valley. Untroubled by the usual mass of people in high season, you can appreciate the splendid and natural beauty of the Valle de Ordesa along this cool and shady path.

At the **Puente de la Glera** follow the sign to Camino Turieto and walk along the Río Ara to the end of the drivable track where the actual Camino Turieto begins. The broad path continues close to the river through fenced meadows and soon reaches a fork where a path turns off to the Puente de los Navarros and into the Valle de Bujaruelo. Keep straight on along the red and white marked path which gets narrower and slowly ascends up through a wood. The vertical rock faces of the Peña Duáscaro are now on your

The imposing rock prow of Tozal del Mallo.

right-hand side. Ignore the path branching off left at another junction and go directly across the park boundary. The path slowly bends round into the Valle de Ordesa and on the left-hand side of the path there's a safety wall beside the steeply sloping valley hillside. It's worth lingering a while to enjoy the view: below, the Río Arazas plunges down the divided Cascada de Molinieto and the monumental rocks of Mondarruego, Tozal del Mallo and Gallinero tower up into the sky opposite. Continue walking through a marvellous beech wood, past a wooden shelter, then a short detour makes a closer view possible of the Cascada de Tomborrotera which cascades in a fan shape down into a green pool. Join the main path again and after a stabilised section of path there's another detour you can take to a viewing balcony over the Cascada de Abetos. A little later on, a path turns off left to the river and to the Puente de Ordesa where there's a memorial to the French photographer Lucien Briet. The GR crosses over onto the opposite side of the river, but you remain for a while on the beaten path with a view of the imposing Tobacor canyon walls and walk through expansive river meadows with a thin stand of trees until you reach a crossroads with several signposts. The **Pradera de Ordesa**, 1300m, lies on the other side of the Río Arazas and is the classic starting point for walks into the Ordesa valley. A large car park fills the area today. Go across the bridge if you want to catch the bus back.

15 Through the Valle de Ordesa

Classic ramble through the spectacular canyon

Pradera de Ordesa – Puente de Soaso – Refugio de Góriz and back

Location: Torla, 1030m.
Starting point: Pradera de Ordesa, 1300m.
Walking times: Pradera de Ordesa – Puente de Soaso 3 hrs.; Puente de Soaso – Refugio de Góriz 1-1½ hrs. (depending on which option you take); return 3½ hrs.; total time 8 hrs.
Difference in height: 450m (as far as Puente de Soaso), 900m to Refugio de Góriz.
Grade: a very long walk (8km), but which is not difficult in terms of the route-finding and the gradient until you get to the head of the valley. Steep ascent from the Circo de Soaso with two options: a) direct path up through the steep head of the valley with a lengthy secured passage (Clavijas de Soaso) of stakes and chains; some climbing experience, sure-footedness and a lack of vertigo essential. b) Camino de las Mulas: easier, but longer way round on a zigzag path on the right-hand slope of the valley. GR path, marked red and white.
Recommended map: Ordesa y Monte Perdido, 1:25,000 (Parques Nacionales de España 1); published by Ministerio de Fomento, 2000.
Stops and accommodation: bars and restaurants in Torla; bar in the Pradera de Ordesa (only in summer); Refugio de Góriz, be sure to book meals and accommodation beforehand, ✆ 974 34 21 01.
Tip: the drive to the Pradera de Ordesa is closed off in Easter week and in the summer. There's a shuttle bus from Torla (see information on 'Getting there').
Alternative: return from the Cascada de Arripas along the little used roadway on the left-hand side of the river. At a signpost for Regreso al Aparcamiento, a forest track turns off down to the bridge over the Río Arazas. Cross over onto the other side and return along the roadway keeping close to the river almost all of the time. The path later on runs through the delightful valley and meets a fork with several signposts. Go right here across the bridge to the car park.

At the head of the Valle de Ordesa (Circo de Soasa).

It's not without good reason that the Valle de Ordesa is the most visited natural attraction in the Pyrenees. If possible you should try to avoid the throngs of people in August so that you can enjoy this uniquely beautiful landscape in total peace and quiet. The spectacular backdrop of the high towering rock faces of the canyon and its steep side valleys as well as the spectacle of the Río Arazas with its dramatic waterfalls, series of ledges and the broad waterfall at the head of the valley provide you with an unforgettable experience. Most visitors turn back at the Circo de Soaso, but if you are a confident walker, you can extend this walk with an ascent to the Refugio de Góriz at the foot of Monte Perdido and its sister peaks. The hut, which is staffed all year round, is the starting point for alpine mountain walks in and around the Marboré massif, especially the regular ascents of Monte Perdido and Brecha de Rolando.

The start of the Camino Soaso is at the end of the **car park** through a mixed wood. Walk along the left bank of the Río Arazas up the valley and after a

statue of the Virgin Mary the path branches off left to the Circo de Cotatuero cliffs where an impressive waterfall plunges into the depths. Stay on the valley path which is dominated by the fantastic rock faces of Tobacor towering up into the sky.

After you have gone through the Barranco de las Ollas you come past a spring on the left of the path (Fuente de Arripas) and a few paces further on you can make a short detour to a look-out over the Cascada de Arripas. Back on the track, go up round some bends which bring you closer to the narrow cleft of the river which thunders down two huge cliffs in quick succession – the Cascadas de la Cueva and del Estrecho. You can get a closer view of the two waterfalls from the viewing balconies.

The path continues swiftly uphill for a while longer and you walk through a fairytale beech wood, past a wooden shelter. Immediately the roadway starts to level out and in one steep narrowing of the valley it is even cut into the rock. The wood gradually thins out and you walk along beside the river through the open valley with its vast sub-alpine meadows. Then the roadway ends and becomes a comfortable hiking trail which is also stabilised here and there. Past a second shelter you come to a signpost drawing your attention to the Gradas de Soaso. The valley bottom gets narrower again here and you ascend quickly up round some bends by the side of crystal clear water broadly flowing over delightful steps and ledges. Then the valley opens out and you walk through the wonderful pastureland where the river gently meanders.

With a view of the wide head of the valley, the Circo de Soaso, above which the Tres Sorores tower majestically, walk towards the broadly fanned Cascada Cola de Caballo. Before the waterfall you arrive at the **Puente de Soaso**, 1750m. Cross over onto the other side of the river on the bridge and you now have to choose between the two alternatives for the ascent up the rock faces. The signposted path to the 'Clavijas' goes up across the face to the foot of the conspicuously eroded steep wall where the narrow path in the rock begins, secured with iron stakes and chains. At the top it meets the Camino de las Mulas which surmounts the scree-covered eastern slope of the valley basin round long bends.

After the two paths have joined, follow the red and white waymarkings, walk across the terrace on the slope, approach the deep cleft of the gorge of the Río Arazas, climb the bend up round a second distinct cliff edge, and soon afterwards a third and then you reach some flatter levels. The gorge slowly bends round to the left while your path keeps ascending comfortably in a northerly direction and reaches the **Refugio de Góriz**, 2195m, without any further difficulties.

The Río Arazas offers a dramatic spectacle with a fantastic series of ledges (Gradas de Soaso).

16 Punta Cuta, 2240m

Valle de Ordesa 'seen from the air'

Torla – Miradores del Molar – Collado Diazas – Punta Cuta and back

Location: Torla, 1030m.
Starting point: barrier on the track to the Sierra de las Cutas, 1200m. Beyond Torla you turn right to the Río Ara campsite as far as the Puente de Glera across the Río Ara. Immediately after the bridge continue left along the track by the side of the river and there's a right-hand bend after about a kilometre. Continue to the barrier.
Walking times: starting point – Miradores del Molar 2¼ hrs.; Miradores del Molar – Collado Diazas ¾ hr.; Collado Diazas – Punta Cuta ½ hr.; return 2¾ hrs.; total time 6¼ hrs.

Difference in height: 1040m.
Grade: technically easy walk, but with a large variation in height. PR path (marked yellow and white) and roadway. The ascent to Punta Cuta is without paths, but you can't get lost.
Shady forest path at first, then open ground to the end.
Recommended map: Ordesa y Monte Perdido, 1:25,000 (Parques Nacionales de España 1); published by Ministerio de Fomento, 2000.
Stops and accommodation: bars and restaurants in Torla.

Punta Cuta is not a summit experience in the strict sense of the word, but in recompense, the view from the easy 'peak' is a real enjoyment and difficult to beat. The thousand metre deeply-fissured Valle de Ordesa and its huge canyon walls are a spectacular sight with an infinite number of nuances in form and colour, while the distant view of the Valle de Bujaruelo across the Brecha de Rolando reaches as far as Cotiella.

Take the path marked yellow and white at the **barrier** which branches off left (from the direction of travel) and ascends round gentle bends up through a dense mixed wood. Cross over the track several times and after ¾ of an hour you come to the Ermita de Santa Ana which lies at the edge of a terraced slope. The path immediately leaves the track again behind the Ermita (signposted Miradores del Molar) and ascends the ridge between gorse and solitary trees, briefly meets the track and then immediately goes away from it again. At another fork keep on the right (yellow and white waymarkings on trees) and continue up the slope at a gradual in-
cline through pine forest. The path
brings you closer to the roadway
and ends there, and you continue
to the left, past a small spring at the
right-hand edge of the roadway.
After some sharp bends you come
to a signpost to the Miradores
which leads you to the left towards
the first of the **Miradores del**

On the way to Punta Cuta..

Molar, 1990m. The view from the balconies high above the Ordesa valley gives you a foretaste of the fabulous summit view which awaits you on the Punta Cuta. Back on the roadway follow it again as it gently goes uphill. You can find some easy shortcuts across the wide sweeping bends. Punta Diazas rises up ahead which, from the Miradores, had appeared like a conspicuous protruding tooth of rock. The roadway keeps to the foot of the steep wooded slope and Punta Cuta whose pointed shape is in striking contrast to the precipitous projection of Punta Diazas. The Collado de Diazas dips quite visibly between the two summits. Leave the roadway in good time and walk towards the col near near to which the extremely steep Senda de los Cazadores emerges from the Ordesa valley. At the **Collado de Diazas**, 2145m, turn eastwards and climb without paths along the rock-strewn and not overly steep ridge directly up to Punta Cuta, 2240m. If you still have enough stamina you can make another detour to Punta Diazas on the return and enjoy the view from the two Miradores situated there. It can also be easily and quickly reached along the moderately inclined ridge from the Collado.

17 Faja de Pelay, 2000m

Along the classic mountain path through the Valle de Ordesa

Pradera de Ordesa – Mirador de Calzilarruego – Puente de Soaso and back along the valley path

Location: Torla, 1030m.
Starting point: Pradera de Ordesa, 1300m.
Walking times: Pradera de Ordesa – Mirador de Calzilarruego 1½ hrs., Mirador de Calzilarruego – Puente de Soaso 2½ hrs; return along the valley path 2½ hrs.; total time 6½ hrs.
Difference in height: 700m.
Grade: lengthy walk and as regards fitness, not to be underestimated; long and steep ascent to the Faja de Pelay; comfortable path from there along a predominantly broad ledge with some short exposed sections. The climb up to the *faja* and the second half of the valley path are shady. Be careful: the path on the Faja de Pelay can be dangerous if there's snow and ice when you are advised against it! Check it out with the park wardens.

Recommended map: Ordesa y Monte Perdido, 1:25,000 (Parques Nacionales de España 1); published by Ministerio de Fomento, 2000.
Stops and accommodation: restaurants in Torla; bar in the Pradera de Ordesa (only in summer).
Tip: you should do the walk in the direction in which it is described here since the descent from the *faja* into the valley at the end of the walk would rob you of too much energy. An early start is recommended, so as not to be caught by a storm on the *faja*. The drive to the Pradera de Ordesa is closed off in summer. There is a shuttle bus from Torla. (see information on 'Getting there').
Linking Tip: possible to link with Walk 15 (ascent to the Refugio de Góriz).

The wonderful steep walls of the Valle de Ordesa are divided many times by narrow balconies and terraces on the slope running high up in the rock. Some of these *fajas* are passable and offer you incomparable scenic views. The Faja de Pelay on the southern walls of the valley is the longest; six hundred metres high above the glittering band of the Río Arazas you walk as far as the head of the valley, always accompanied by the majestic scenery of the canyons. The return along the valley path rounds off this walk with a truly brilliant experience.

In the **Pradera de Ordesa** go to the end of the car park and follow the signpost to the Senda de los Cazadores. Cross over the Río Arazas on the bridge and a little further along you come to a signposted crossroads where the Senda de los Cazadores continues straight ahead – a former hunters' path which led into the high shooting area for chamois and ibex. As you go past a warning sign 'Senda muy peligrosa. Hielo y aludes' (very dangerous path. Ice and avalanches) the path starts to

View from the Faja de Pelay.

demand a high level of fitness. It now climbs six hundred metres up round a series of bends across the steep slopes through a beech wood. By the time you reach a fork in the path the largest part of the ascent is over. Leave the Senda de los Cazadores here which ascends straight on to the Collado de Diazas and turn off left, climb round the wall of rock rising up in front of you and then reach the walled **Mirador de Calzilarruego**, 2000m, from where the canyon can be seen as if from a bird's eye view. The *refugio* of the same name next to the viewing terrace is unfortunately in a bad state of repair. The Faja de Pelay starts where the path now runs for a long while almost on the level, and only occasionally comes very close to the edge of the sheer cliffs or crosses steep cirques of scree. The walk is more like a stroll through fantastic scenery where you are constantly inspired to stop and enjoy the views.

After a good hour you come past an open shelter (Refugio de Abé), then the *faja* sweeps round to the north-east and broadens out into a gorgeous terrace with meadows, flowers and a thin stand of trees while you head for the enormous valley basin of Circo de Soaso above which rise the towering Tres Sorores – Cilindro, Monte Perdido and Soum de Ramond. The path slowly descends into the valley and divides into two paths far below in the stony ground – a bridle path round long bends begins on the right-hand side which goes over the precipitous head of the valley and leads to the Refugio de Góriz (see Walk 15), but stay on the path branching down to the Río Arazas until you arrive at the **Puente de Soaso**, 1750m, at the foot of the broadly fanned Cascada Cola de Caballo. Take the path on the other side of the river, which brings you back to the Pradera de Ordesa (see Walk 15).

18 Faja de las Flores, 2450m

The path along the the balcony of superlatives – unique!

Pradera de Ordesa – Faja de las Flores – Pradera de Ordesa

Location: Torla, 1030m.

Starting point: Pradera de Ordesa, 1300m.

Walking times: Pradera de Ordesa – start of the Faja de las Flores 3½ hrs.; path along the Faja de las Flores 2 hrs.; end of the Faja de las Flores – Pradera de Ordesa 2¾ hrs.; total time 8¼ hrs.

Difference in height: 1150m.

Grade: long and demanding walk only for experienced mountain walkers; lack of vertigo, sure-footedness and some climbing experience absolutely essential. Very steep ascents and descents, some exposed paths and narrow tracks. On the ascent through the Circo de Carriata there are shorter sections of climbing which are made safe with iron stakes (Clavijas de Cotatuero); an alternative way round goes along an airy balcony only half of which is secured with a chain. On the descent of the Circo de Cotatuero there's a short, but very exposed crossing on the steep wall to be overcome, but it is secured with iron stakes and in places, a chain (Clavijas de Cotatuero), but a few metres that has not been made safe have good foot and hand holds.

Be careful: this walk is extremely dangerous in rain, snow and ice!

Recommended map: Ordesa y Monte Perdido, 1:25,000 (Parques Nacionales de España 1); published by Ministerio de Fomento, 2000.

Stops and accommodation: restaurants in Torla; bar in the Pradera de Ordesa (only in summer)

Tips: the drive to the Pradera de Ordesa is closed off in summer. There's a shuttle bus from Torla (see information on 'Getting there').

Alternative: Tozal del Mallo, 2250m: marvellous look-out post with spectacular views; the Tozal del Mallo is also an alternative destination in its own right. After the Clavijas de Carriata the path runs along a broad sloping ledge, called Rincón de Salarons. Follow here the obvious grassy path to the west. It stays close to the cliff edge, runs round some partly exposed recesses and then bends towards the more recently formed ridge of the Tozal del Mallo, which you climb southwards up to the rounded summit. Total time there and back from the Rincón de Salarons 1½ hrs.; as an individual walk 6½ hrs.

The Faja de las Flores is an absolute dream of a walk, but not for those with weak nerves. The daring balcony goes along dizzying heights above the valley floor across the vertical walls of Punta Gallinero. Together with the breathtaking views far across the valley there are exciting and scenically spectacular ascents and descents in the rock basins of Carriata and Cotatuero. Even if the path along the Faja de las Flores is less exposed and narrow than it at first seems, nevertheless sure-footedness and a lack of vertigo are absolutely necessary, and in addition there's a very exposed section on the open rock to be negotiated on the descent.

From the **Pradera de Ordesa** walk back along the approach road for about 1km as far as the Casa Oliván (old information hut) where your walk begins at the signpost for Circo de Carriata / Tozal del Mallo. The path immediately

The Faja de las Flores runs as a horizontal ledge across the vertical rock.

enters a dense mixed wood and continues uphill. As you go up round some bends you pass a wooden shelter and soon afterwards the path becomes rocky terrain covered in gorse. The Circo de Carriata opens up ahead and the curious monumental rock of Tozal del Mallo rises up opposite. You come to a fork where you follow the sign to Tozal del Mallo / Clavijas de Carriata, cross the streambed and walk along the gently ascending path westwards towards the steep rock face of Tozal del Mallo. Then the path changes course a little and winds up the grassy slope. At a second signpost with the same inscription, the path makes an about-face and crosses the slope to the north-east ascending to the foot of a rock wall which runs through the Circo. With a bit of easy scrambling you climb up the stepped rock where there are cairns to help the route-finding, and afterwards you follow the furrowed path uphill round some steep bends. At the next fork with a red marked wooden stick, continue right along the now relatively flat path which soon becomes a really narrow strip at the foot of a rock face. Turn into a recess along the airy path and head towards the small stream. Be careful here: do not cross over the stream, but shortly before it you have to climb 10m higher up across the rocky slope to the left beside cairns to the wooden signpost for Clavijas/Fajeta. The path divides here and further up joins the Rincón de Salarons again. Take the path to the Paso de la Fajeta and follow it to the right. It quickly becomes a broad strip of ledge, at first

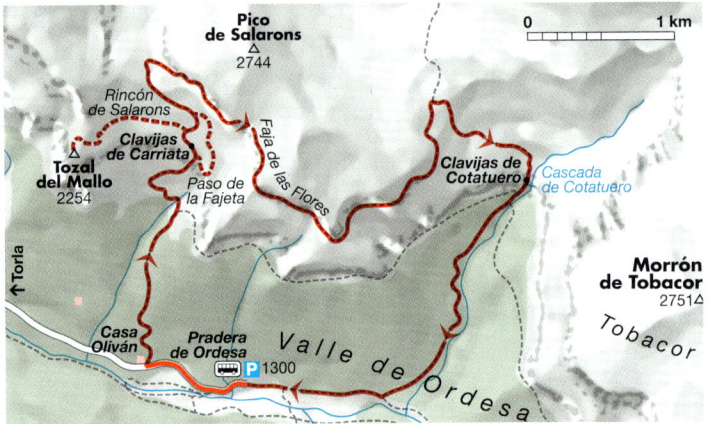

secured with a handrail, which goes round a wall projection and then into the steep *barranco*. Now the path becomes more exposed and has no more protection. Cairns indicate the easy climbing route on the left up over little rock steps and ledges.

Do not follow the obvious path to the Clavijas which continues left at the fork, in stead climb up a little bit further following the cairns and you come to another junction where you keep right. The first iron stakes are already visible and a little further above and a few metres to the left, follow the actual Clavijas de Carriata, which make the climbing of the rock cleft decidedly easier. Then a little bit more scrambling on a rock cliff and you come onto a sloping ledge, the Rincón de Salarons, where the Paso de la Fajeta path emerges over on the right. (To the left a narrow path goes over to the Tozal del Mallo, see Alternative). From here the Faja de las Flores can be seen easily: it runs like a horizontal cut across the steep rock below the slope of the Punta Gallinero. Continue climbing up the slope on the beaten path, come through meadows with boulders, go round a rock pedestal which has a large cairn on the top and eventually walk a little way to the west through a stony area until you have reached the entrance onto the **Faja de las Flores**, 2450m. There's another boulder field at the start, then it quickly becomes narrower and filters into the rock. After walking for a few minutes you come to an enormous boulder leaning against the steep rock face – an unmistakable indication that you are on the right path.

Without losing height you now go round the Punta Gallinero along the balcony, constantly going in and out of huge recesses in the rock, changing the direction of your views and orientation. At a bulge in the *faja* with a large boulder (a nice place to stop for a rest) turn into the Circo de Cotatuero. Walk further into the huge rock basin (beside the path there are loads of edelweiss) and eventually you reach a stony area. On the right below you lies a green plateau, with a stream running through it, with an abrupt sheer drop which plunges down the cliffs of the Circo. This plateau is your next objective. Along the north-wards leading path you enter an increasingly more defined limestone region. Several gullies descend on your right and drop down to the plateau. There's no lack of cairns here, in fact they are rather confusing, but for a while you stay on the beaten path and do not turn off until you reach a rock corridor which is quite conspicuous with its larger cairns and tracks. Descend down this without any difficulty to the plateau and there the path to

The Faja de las Flores.

the entrance to the cirque becomes obvious again. Well-placed cairns on the right of the waterfall go beside the stepped rock faces down as far as the Clavijas de Cotatuero.

At first the horizontal traverse is made safe with chains and rungs, but then there are a few metres without any protection and again iron stakes aid the short climb down a cleft. Then you are once more on firm ground and you quickly follow the path down some zigzags to a shelter (Abrigo de Cotatuero) close to the bridge over the torrent and from there continue along the forest path with a speedy descent into the valley where you meet the broad valley path. Follow this right and in a few minutes you are back at the Pradera de Ordesa.

19 Monte Perdido, 3335m

Onto the popular peak of the Pyrenees

Refugio de Góriz – Lago Helado – Monte Perdido and back

Location: Torla, 1030m.
Starting point: Refugio de Góriz, 2195m.
Walking times: Refugio de Góriz – Lago Helado 2½ hrs; Lago Helado – Monte Perdido 1 hr.; return 3 hrs.; total time 6½ hrs.
Difference in height: 1140m.
Grade: high alpine walk only for experienced mountain walkers; steep sections of path, easy sections of climbing (I). In the large labyrinth of boulders you need to have a good sense of direction. Very strenuous ascent of the so-called 'Escupidera', a steep (35°) ramp with small scree below the summit (walking poles would be an advantage). Be careful: most accidents occur on the Escupidera as a result of not having the correct gear for snow and ice; there is a chance of finding snow even in high summer when crampons and ice axes are essential! The hut wardens of the Refugio de Góriz will also give you details of the conditions over the phone. The south ascent described here is generally considered to be an 'easy' walk which in optimum conditions, is certainly the case. Nevertheless you

should not underestimate the fact that you are walking in high mountains with all the resulting dangers. Pay special attention, therefore, to adequate gear and stable weather conditions.
Recommended map: Ordesa y Monte Perdido, 1:25,000 (Parques Nacionales de España 1); published by Ministerio de Fomento, 2000.
Stops and accommodation: bars and restaurants in Torla; bar in the Pradera de Ordesa (only in summer); Refugio de Góriz, telephone in advance for meals and accommodation, ✆ 974 34 12 01; the hut is hopelessly overfull in summer.
Tips: ascent to the Refugio de Góriz, see Walk 15. An interesting alternative is also offered by the shuttle buses which bring mountaineers from Torla and Nerín along the track to the Sierra de las Cutas to the Mirador de Ziarrazils. From there you can walk in just under two hours along the GR path, waymarked in red and white, keeping to the edge of the canyon all the way to the Refugio de Góriz. Information, up-to-date timetables and reservations at the tourist information.

The name of Monte Perdido conjures up myths and the love of nature. It plays a central role in the history of mountaineering in the Pyrenees and today it is, for many people, a cult mountain that you have to have climbed, just like many of the peaks in the Alps. As mountains go, Monte Perdido does not exactly have what you would call a beautiful shape and in that respect, the neighbouring peaks of Cilindro and Soum de Ramond have more to offer. But set into the surrounding dramatic landscape of rocks, it unfolds a magic which so fascinated its first ascender, Louis Ramond, that he compared it to Mont Blanc: if you have seen the king of the granite mountains, you should also see the king of the limestone mountains!
At the **Refugio de Góriz**, go over to the nearby weather station where the well-trodden path begins to ascend. In a north-easterly direction round some short bends it crosses the grassy slopes which are also interrupted by

small rocky ledges. Faded way-markings and cairns leave you no doubt as to which route to take. The path soon winds round to the north and goes over a small rock step after which the ground levels out again. Climb up towards a rock face which bends round the corner onto the broad slope of the Barranco de Góriz. The increasingly stonier path brings you to the foot of the rock face, and you continue to climb parallel to it uphill and arrive at a fork marked with cairns which continues on the right in the steep scree corridor. The route descends here to the Soum de Ramond, the south-eastern neighbouring peak of Monte Perdido, but you continue along the path at the foot of the rock face which, in between times, goes below overhanging rock until you reach a rocky projection which requires some easy climbing. The path turns off briefly, but then turns back towards the huge rock step that continues right across the slope. This has been visible for a long while on the approach path.

View from the summit of the Lago Helado and Cilindro.

75

Ascent to Monte Perdido in winter.

A moraine field on the left ahead stretches down the slope. The path now bends to the north-west and heads for the boulders which you cross going north. You need to keep a regular look out on the way so as not to lose your sense of direction, because the numerous cairns do not always give the best route through the chaos of boulders. What's important is that you do not go across the floor of the valley, but keep on the right-hand side of the *barranco*.

After you have left the confusion of rocks you still have to make the climb up the steep ledge of the valley. Once at the top you find yourself standing above the circular **Lago Helado**, 2980m, which fills out the scree trough at the foot of Cilindro. The rock wall of the Collado Cilindro sweeps up on the other side of the lake which allows you to cross over to the Balcón de Pineta. On your right the Escupidera runs down from the summit of Monte Perdido. The path makes a sharp bend to the south-east, first ascends along the ridge on the right of the gully and further up swings onto the steep ramp up which you now zigzag steeply. Several tracks lead uphill, but you can often make better progress on the firm scree next to the well-trodden and 'slippery' tracks.

The strenuous ascent ends on the flat col at the foot of the rounded summit of Monte Perdido. The path here bends to the south and climbs the last vertical metres to the summit of **Monte Perdido**, 3335m, where a breathtaking view in all directions awaits you.

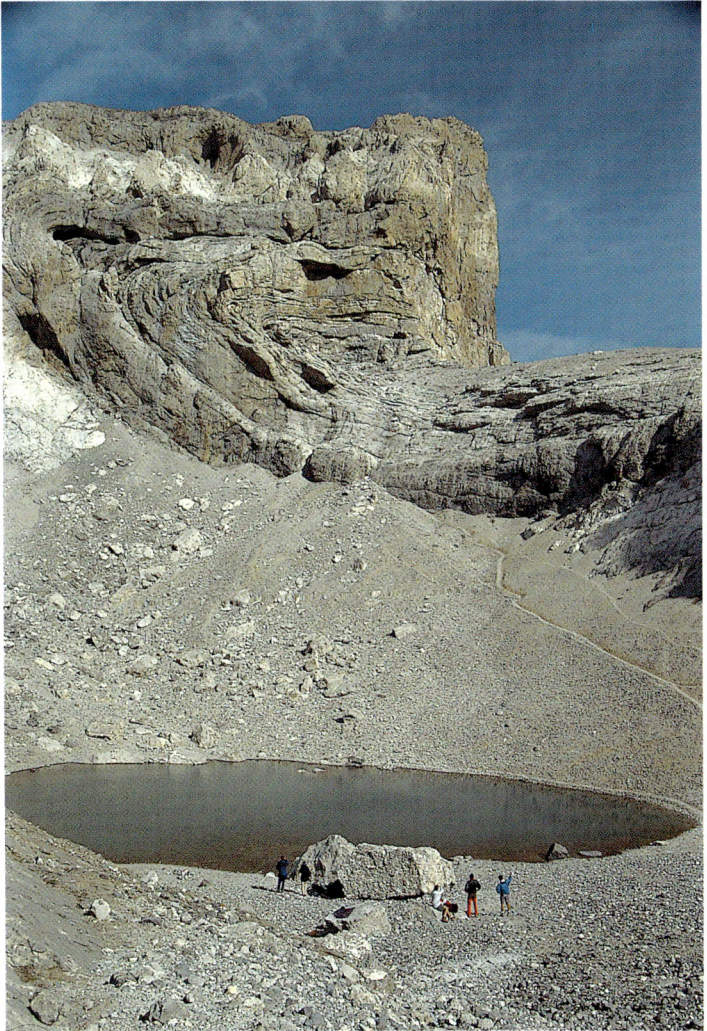

The circular Lago Helado and the misshapen rock of Cilindro.

20 Cañón de Añisclo

Huge rock faces, luxuriant vegetation, thundering waterfalls and green pools – an enjoyable walk through the famous canyon

Puente San Úrbez – La Ripareta and back

Location: Escalona, 600m; Sarvisé, 860m.

Starting point: car park at the entrance to the Cañón de Añisclo near the Puente San Úrbez, 980m. Coming from Escalona drive through the Desfiladero de las Cambras, from Sarvisé via Fanlo and past Nerín

Walking times: Puente San Úrbez – La Ripareta 2 ¾ hrs.; return 2¼ hrs.; total time 5 hrs.

Difference in height: 440m.

Grade: easy walk on roadway and stabilised hiking trail; very shady.

Recommended map: Ordesa y Monte Perdido, 1:25,000 (Parques Nacionales de España 1); published by Ministerio de Fomento, 2000.

Stops and accommodation: bars and restaurants in Escalona and Sarvisé; bar in Buerba and Fanlo.

Tips: the drive from Escalona is regulated during Easter week and in the summer (see information on 'Getting there').

Alternative: if you want to extend the walk, then the adjoining walk to the Fuen Blanca can be recommended: the valley path continues behind La Ripareta on the left of the Río Bellos through dense vegetation, and alternates between inclines and flatter stretches. Just before the Barranco de Capradiza flowing in from the left a path leads across a bridge onto the opposite bank, ascends round bends and comes to a signposted fork where a stabilised path goes up on the right to the high plateaus of the canyon. Keep straight ahead, immediately cross a small torrent from the right and a little further on, the path narrows at a steep drop on the slope and slowly descends to the river. Walk along beside the Río Bellos through the valley as it opens out to a bridge with a fork, 1700m. The destination of the walk (there and back from La Ripareta 2¾ hrs.). The Barranco Fuen Blanca runs in on the left and the Fuen Blanca spring emerges as a large waterfall on the left above in the rock. The path continues straight on to the Collado de Añisclo (see Walk 31, alternative), it climbs the Barranco Fuen Blanca up to the left and leads across the Collado Arrablo to the Refugio de Göriz, (see Walk 15). The Refugio de Fuen Blanca lies 15 mins. away (self-catering hut for 4-6 people): cross over the river on the bridge and follow the path heading for the spring which runs directly past the hut.

The Cañón de Añisclo forms the longest valley cleft in the National Park. Going from the Collado de Añisclo it eats its way deeper and deeper into the limestone plateau as far as the exit to the valley which is enclosed by the steep cliffs of Mondoto and Sestrales. There's an abundance of scenic impressions awaiting the walker between the thousand metre high rock faces along the dramatic Río Bellos, as if nature had put itself on show. The French photographer called the famous canyon 'an unending, geological poem' and this is no exaggeration.

From the car park go down the street for a few metres, turn left into the closed roadway and straight away you are at the **Puente de San Úrbez**,

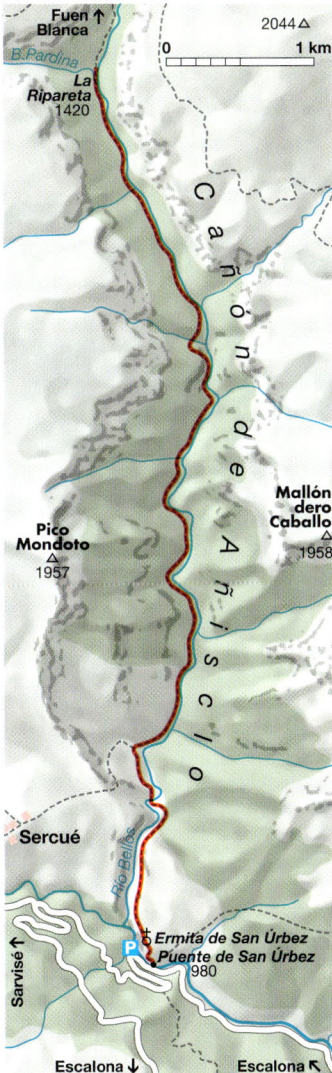

The steep cliffs of Sestrales.

which spans the dark and narrow gorge at a dizzying height. This architectural master piece dates from the 18th century and is a little devalued by the new and wide bridge right next to it.

After you have crossed the Río Bellos on one of the two bridges, the broad roadway runs into the gorge. Follow the roadway and come past the Ermita de San Úrbez set into the rock. Gradually you get closer and closer to the level of the river while the cliffs of Mondoto tower up opposite.

At the concreted Puente de Sangons change over onto the other bank. The roadway ends and becomes a hiking path along which you slowly gain height.

Leave the GR path turning off left to Sercué (see Walk 21) behind you, the forest gets thicker and thicker and you walk through this from now on to the end of the walk. The Río Bellos flows way below and now and then the gorge allows you a view of the thundering waterfalls and beautifully shaped pools. At a

Entrance to the Cañón de Añisclo.

conspicuous turning the path brings you closer to the river which runs here through the flat, smooth rocky banks. With a pleasant gradual gradient you cross over some side streams. The gorge then gets narrower and the valley slope ahead becomes so steep that the path veers round to the side up a strenuous incline.

Moving away from the river you now quickly ascend facing down the valley. After you have gained a fair bit of height, the path curves back the other way and goes up the valley, from now on more on the level. You soon reach an open viewing platform which gives you a splendid view of the gigantic rock walls of Sestrales and its vertically steep gorges on the other side of the Río Bellos.

On the last section of the walk the path keeps on the same level and you stroll through a marvellous beech wood and eventually come to **La Ripareta**, 1420m, the wide mouth of the Barranco Pardina flowing in from the left. This idyllic spot on the flat rocky banks of the Río Bellos provides the opportunity for an ample rest.

The Río Bellos has many marvellous waterfalls.

21 Valley and mountain walk around the Cañón de Añisclo

Isolated paths and surprising variety in landscape

Mallarguero bridge – Sercué – Cañón de Añisclo – Faja Barranco Viandico – Cueva de los Moros – Mallarguero bridge

Location: Escalona, 600m; Sarvisé, 860m.
Starting point: bridge across the Mallarguero, 1050m. From Escalona drive through the Desfiladero de las Cambras, past the car park at the Cañón de Añisclo and continue as far as the fork in the road. Go straight on here in the direction of Fanlo/Nerín as far as the bridge with the signpost Sercué. From Sarvisé via Fanlo, keep going straight on at the turn-off to Nerín, continue over the Río Aso and as far as the bridge.
Walking times: total time for the round walk, 3 hrs.
Difference in height: 250m.

Grade: easy walk on comfortable footpaths, sometimes a GR path (marked red and white); only the path to the Faja des Barranco Viandico is rather unclear.
Recommended map: Ordesa y Monte Perdido, 1:25,000 (Parques Nacionales de España 1); published by Ministerio de Fomento, 2000.
Stops and accommodation: restaurants in Escalona and Sarvisé, bar in Buerba, Nerín and Fanlo.
Tips: the drive from Escalona is regulated during Easter week and in the summer (see information on 'Getting there').
Linking Tip: can be combined with Walk 20.

A walk could hardly be more diverting or more varied. This little-known round walk gives you a marvellous impression of the scenic diversity and surprises you with several changes in perspectives. At first it goes up to the abandoned little village of Sercué on the ridge of Mondoto, then along a well contrived path across steep cliffs down to the Añisclo canyon, along the Río Bellos and eventually along a hidden *faja* path above the Viandico gorge to the exit of a cave.

At the **bridge** across the Barranco Mallarguero follow the signpost to Sercué. Along the gently descending path between box trees and pines you quickly come to the pretty Puente de la Espucialla, which spans a narrowing of the Río Aso. The path continues on the right on the other side and quickly ascends, sometimes over rock steps, and soon leads away from the gorge. The hill, on which Sercué lies hidden between trees, comes quickly into view. The path turns northwards (ignore the paths running straight on at the foot of the hill), heads at first towards the western facing slope, then bends sharply to the right and goes up the south slope. Stone walls at the edge of the path and neglected terraces anticipate the village of **Sercué**, 1140m. You come past a first hut with a threshing floor from where there are beautiful views, then past some more huts and derelict houses. Go through

The faja path through the Río Aso gorge.

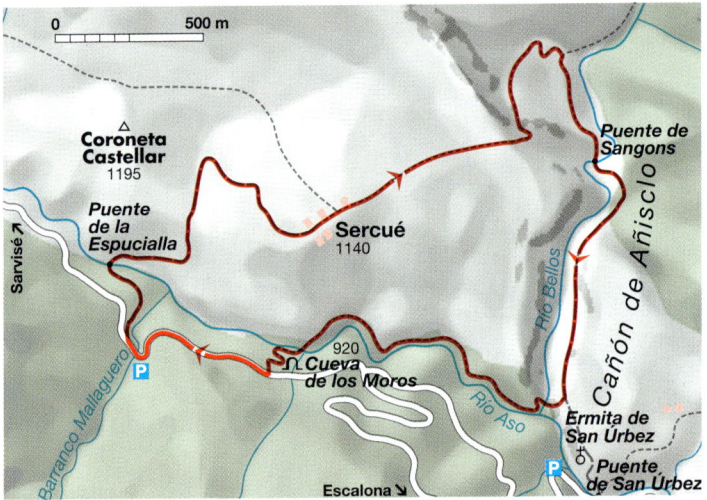

the abandoned hamlet on the main path and join the GR path coming across from Nerín.

At a fork behind the village keep right and walk along the gently descending path directly towards the edge of the canyon. The sweeping cliffs of Mondoto come more and more into view and you pass the park boundary (information board) and afterwards a small cleft after which begins the descent to the Río Bellos.

Along the path running up the valley short steps alternate with flat sections and then the path zigzags quickly down to the floor of the valley. Take the right-hand path at a fork and after a few paces join the broad valley path of the **Cañón de Añisclo**, 1000m, which you now follow to the right. This soon becomes a roadway which changes over onto the left-hand bank of the Río Bellos at the Puente de Sangons.

Follow the river for a while until you come to some signposts where you take the right-hand path turning off right back down to the Río Bellos and cross the river on the wooden bridge. At the next fork immediately afterwards keep on the left and climb up a short steep section. Then the path bends round to the right into the gorge of the Río Aso. A few metres before a large display of stratification, directly at a Parque Nacional sign, leave the path and take an unclear path which goes steeply up the slope on the right to the foot of the spectacularly coloured steep rock face where the path, once more obvious, begins along the **Faja Barranco Viandico**, 950m. The

84

narrow path subsequently varies little in height. Walk along the bottom of the beautiful rock faces high above the river and through a dense stand of trees protecting you from the drop.

Eventually the path brings you closer to the river and ends on the right-hand bank above some narrow rapids. Walk along the easily passable rocky bank a little further up the river until you reach a series of large boulders in the water on which you can cross the Río Aso even when there's a strong current (nevertheless, take care – the rock can be wet and slippery).

On the opposite bank you now walk a few paces up the river and you immediately meet the streambed of the **Cueva de los Moros**, 920m, the mouth of which is hidden a few metres higher up on the dense wooded slope. The cave stream has often dried up in summer. The exit to the cave is covered in loam and very low. Just on the other side of the streambed there's a wonderful pool of the Río Aso which is an inviting place for a swim (very cold spring water). The forest path begins here as well, up to the road where you go right and after another 500m, reach your starting point at the bridge.

Exit from the Cueva de los Moros.

22 Pico Mondoto, 1960m

Spectacular walk to the western cliffs of the Añisclo canyon

Nerín – Pico Mondoto and back

Location: Nerín, 1280m.
Starting point: water depot at Nerín, 1350m. Take the track branching off right just before Nerín as far as the barrier with the wardens' hut, park there.
Walking times: car park – Pico Mondoto 2 hrs.; return 1½ hrs.; total time 3½ hrs.
Difference in height: 610m.
Grade: easy walk on good marked paths (yellow), at the end without paths in places up to the summit. No shade at all.

Recommended map: Ordesa y Monte Perdido, 1:25,000 (Parques Nacionales de España 1); published by Ministerio de Fomento, 2000.
Food and accommodation: bars and restaurants in Nerín.
Tips: the drive from Escalona through the Desfiladero de las Cambras is restricted during Easter week and in the summer (see information on 'Getting there').

The tectonic powers which were at work during the formation of the Marboré massif are displayed most spectacularly at Pico Mondoto. The serrated western flank of the Añisclo canyon appears as if it has broken out of the earth's crust and been thrust upwards. The ridge of this compact mountain, on the other hand, is surprisingly tame and provides you with a leisurely walk up to one of the most impressive viewing points in the National Park.

A little above the **water depot** you will find the waymarker on the rock for

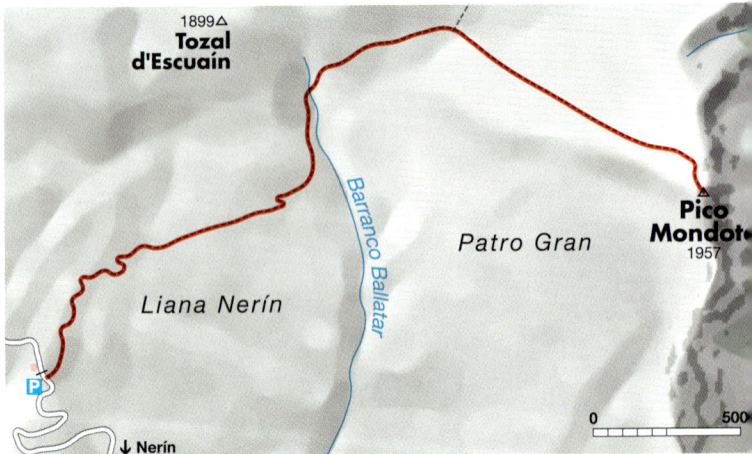

View of the steep cliffs of Sestrales and Pico Mondoto.

Mondoto with an arrow. This is where the walk begins along the sloping path waymarked with yellow dots and cairns. A fork soon follows with another signpost and your path continues here on the right and crosses diagonally to the east the gently inclined slope covered in box trees and gorse. Now walk for quite a while as far as a broad *barranco* coming down from the north which has a broad flat rocky bank on the left. Follow the cairns and waymarkers until you come to a large cairn and a yellow arrow. Change here onto the other side of the *barranco* and climb up the slope along the stony path in a northerly direction. The path gradually merges into grassy slopes with loose small bushes then becomes a narrow path which climbs up to the hollow between Mondoto and Tozal d'Escuaín. The yellow waymarkers change to white, but they become increasingly rare and then stop altogether. Once you have arrived on the ridge of the col your path turns to the east and runs towards the broad strip of grass which is bordered on the right by the rocky cliff. On a little- used track climb up through grass and over rocky slabs towards the steep cliffs in the east, then turn a little to the south and arrive at the highest point of the bowl of steep cliffs, **Pico Mondoto**, 1960m, with a tremendous view. A detour along the steep cliffs is highly recommended where the fabulous formations of the rock faces are displayed from a different perspective.

23 Sestrales Bajo, 2075m

Thrilling ascent to the high plateau above the Añisclo canyon

Puente San Úrbez – Collado de las Puertas – Sestrales Bajo and back

Location: Escalona, 600m; Sarvisé, 860m.

Starting point: car park at the entrance to the Cañón de Añisclo near to the Puente San Úrbez, 980m. Coming from Escalona, drive through the Desfiladero de las Cambras from Sarvisé via Fanlo and past Nerín.

Walking times: Puente San Úrbez – Collado de las Puertas 3½ hrs.; Collado de las Puertas – Sestrales Bajo 1 hr.; return 3 ½ hrs.; total time 8 hrs.

Difference in height: 1095m.

Grade: demanding walk which requires a good degree of fitness and mountain experience. Steep sections and some short easy climbing (I); exposed path at the end and steep ascent in a rock corridor. GR path to start with (marked red and white) then narrow path with waymarkers. Mostly shady. Be careful in rain, snow and ice when the exposed section of the path is dangerous!

Recommended map: Ordesa y Monte Perdido, 1:25,000 (Parques Nacionales de España 1); published by Ministerio de Fomento, 2000.

Stops and accommodation: bars and restaurants in Escalona and Sarvisé; bar in Buerba and Fanlo.

Tips: the drive from Escalona through the Desfiladero de las Cambras is regulated during Easter week and in summer (see information on 'Getting there').

Alternative: Sestrales Alto, 2100m. The walk can be extended up to the highest point of Sestrales. From Sestrales Bajo walk easily along the edge of the cliff faces northwards. A large cairn marks the summit of Sestrales Alto. There and back from Sestrales Bajo, ½ hr.

The high plateau of Sestrales Bajo.

The steep flanks, towers and parapets of Sestrales appear to preclude an ascent onto this fantastic monumental rock. But along an exciting and varied path which makes clever use of ledges, clefts and rock channels, you can reach the long ridge of Sestrales with its characteristic limestone scenery. The views across the Añisclo canyon, the vertical Mondoto cliff faces and the National Park are first class.

Walk along the road at the car park down to the roadway and follow this to the left to the **Puente San Úrbez** and a little bit further on you come to the sign for Bestué por Sestrales where the walk begins. Start up a gentle incline along the GR hiking path between box trees and holm oaks and you soon pass the wonderfully situated Bordas de Aso, which lie hidden on the slope on the left above the path. The ascent gets steeper and you go round some bends on a stabilised path then head towards a long scree slope. Climb up the left edge of this at first and then cross it at the height of the rock

The majestic Sestrales.

corridor. The gradient increases considerably now, first through forest, then again on scree and then once more in dense forest.

The view opens up briefly of the huge walls of the Desfiladero de las Cambras, but the now flatter path soon runs through dense forest again. You pass a small spring in the rock on the left (in high summer it's only running with water after heavy rainfall) and then further ahead the path bends round into a large steep recess and runs along the edge of the precipice towards the vertical rock faces. Cross a streambed, then immediately continue through forest once more and you come to a grass-covered platform on the right of the path with a beautiful view. Soon after that there's a second viewing balcony to the south. There is a fork in the path immediately afterwards. Right goes to Bestué, but you keep on the left and proceed uphill along the narrow path, which gets lost in places, to a steep rocky break, called Canal de Arruto. Go up along the stepped rock and immediately afterwards you come to the small ridge of a col with a cairn and the Parque Nacional sign where your path makes a sharp bend round to the west. You now walk for quite a while practically on the level across a beautifully vegetated terrace on the slope at the foot of magnificent rock faces. After the path begins to ascend again it turns to the north and you keep right at a fork waymarked with cairns and meet a really steep scree

Finally at your destination.

slope which comes down from the Collado de las Puertas. First climb up the scree along some well-trodden tracks, but after a while change over to the edge of the forest on the right where you climb the slope along an easier path up to the rock wall below the conspicuous rock tower. Continue there up the slope to the col round steep bends. You arrive at the **Collado de las Puertas**, 2000m. Going to the left here, scramble easily up the small cliff to a platform with a National Park sign. At the end of the long rock face of Sestrales you can see a large window in the rock with a horizontal lintel. Walk towards it along an obvious narrow path across the grass-covered slope close to the steep rock and soon arrive at a conspicuous corridor in the steep face which allows you to climb up onto the high plateau. Following a few cairns, preferably keeping left further up, it's possible to climb up the steep cleft without any difficulties. Once you have reached the wide high plateau of Sestrales stroll along the gently inclined ridge through meadow grass and over bizarre limestone rocks northwards over to the projecting cliff of **Sestrales Bajo**, 207 m.

24 Sestrales Alto, 2100m

Problem-free walk to the breathtakingly steep cliff faces of the Cañón de Añisclo

Collado de Plana Canal – Sestrales Alto and back

Location: Escalona, 600m.
Starting point: Collado de Plana Canal, 1750m. From Escalona drive past Puertolás, and at the following junction go left (in the direction of Bestué), then along the track branching off right (sign for Montaña de Sensa) for a good 9km as far as the Collado (park boundary and barrier). About 45 minute drive along the track.
Walking times: Collado de Plana Canal – Sestrales Alto 2¼ hrs.; return 1¾ hrs.; total time 4 hrs.
Difference in height: 350m.
Grade: easy walk along narrow paths; partly marked with cairns. Without any shade.
Recommended map: Ordesa y Monte Perdido, to a scale of 1:25,000 (Parques Nacionales de España 1); published by Ministerio de Fomento, 2000.
Stops and accommodation: bars and restaurants in Escalona.
Tip: the track is in a bad state of repair in places, but if you take enough care it can be driven with a normal car.
Alternative: Sestrales Bajo, 2075m: short extension of the walk to the projecting cliffs in the south. Continue along the edge of the precipices, at first a little downhill, then gradually uphill again as far as the next projecting plateau. There and back 1 hr.

The defined limestone around Sestrales Bajo forms a striking and rarely seen landscape which is definitely worth a detour. There are grassy islands in between the eroded limestone and numerous flowers, with some edelweiss amongst them.

Añisclo canyon and Tres Sonores.

If you are looking at the thousand metre high walls of Sestrales from the valley floor, you would hardly imagine that a high plateau extended up on the top with sub-alpine meadows. On this easy walk along the top of breathtakingly sheer cliff faces you can appreciate the amazing contrasts in scenery between the dramatic clefts of the canyon and the backdrop of high mountains around Tres Sorores from the most beautiful perspectives.

At the **Collado de Plana Canal** follow the sign for Sestrales Alto y Bajo beyond the barrier and climb up on the left of the furrowed animal tracks onto the grass-covered elevation of Tozal de la Fueva. From here the path leads diagonally left down the slope to the valley bottom, passes a derelict hut and a National Park sign and then runs onto the small knoll where it bends to the south-west and ascends the long ridge of the elevation ahead. After a large cairn there follows a small area of level ground where a horizontal shortcut branches off left (cairn). However, continue ascending up the slope to a cairn and a National Park sign. Ahead of you the Sestrales drop abruptly down in the big semi-circle of the Barranco de Caballo and you turn south-eastwards, descend close to the cliffs down to the recess of the *barranco* and stay on the well-trodden path at the edge of the sheer drops. Going slowly uphill the path skirts a second large recess and then turns south-westwards and keeps heading, close to the edge of the cliffs, to a National Park sign where a fantastic view awaits you across the undulating high plateau and the huge peaks around Monte Perdido. After a few metres southwards you reach **Sestrales Alto**, 2100m, with a stone tower on the top.

At your destination: Sestrales Alto.

25 Castillo Mayor, 2015m

Up to a perfect look-out post

Puertolás – La Plana – Castillo Mayor and back

Location: Escalona, 600m.
Starting point: junction beyond Puertolás, 1140m. Go left at the junction (in the direction of Bestué) and park immediately beyond at the lay-by on the right.
Walking times: car park – La Plana 2¼ hrs.; La Plana – Castillo Mayor ¾ hr.; return 2½ hrs.; total time 5½ hrs.
Difference in height: 875 m.
Grade: easy walk on well-made path in the first section; the ascent of the limestone slope to the summit has hardly any paths, but there are cairns. Good route-finding and sure-footedness essential. Shade only at the start. Be careful – the sharp edged limestone rock full of fissures is dangerous if there's snow and fog.
Recommended map: Ordesa y Monte de Perdido, 1:25,000 (Parques Nacionales España 1); published by Ministerio de Fomento, 2000.
Stops and accommodation: bars and restaurants in Escalona.
Alternative: instead of the direct ascent from La Plana to the summit you can also follow the path going eastwards and climb the grass-covered, then rock-strewn slope up to the edge of the cliffs. Go north-westwards there in a diagonal line across the limestone slope near to the sheer drops, but not staying too close to the edge when trying to find an easy way round several cracks. Be careful walking along the fissured rock. From La Plana to Castillo Mayor, 1¼ hrs.
Tip: you can combine this alternative with the direct route to make a round walk.

Castillo Mayor is an extraordinary phenomenon in all respects. It's an isolated mountain and doesn't appear to belong to any group of mountains, and with its bizarre shape it is more like a tilted table mountain which is broken at the edge. The contrast between gently sloping high mountain pastures and raw limestone rock, which from a distance glistens like ice, is rarely so pronounced.

From the **car park** walk along the road for about a hundred metres until you reach a shepherds' path branching off right which goes up through abandoned terraces. Lined with little stone walls and box trees it runs onto the eastern cliffs of Castillo Mayor which resembles a ship's prow and then enters a mixed forest after a small meadow and curves round a large bend eastwards. Almost on the level it heads towards the greyish-blue rock faces and then changes into a

Curious scene at the Castillo Mayor.

twisting narrow path which winds deftly up the steep slope. Afterwards the path ascends a strenuous incline again through a mixed wood and joins a sloping meadow where there are only feint tracks. Cross the meadow to a cairn at the edge of the forest opposite where the path becomes more distinct again. The forest quickly thins out and only box trees and cushions of gorse cover the broad steep slope where the path stays relatively wide on the left-hand side of the slope and ascends comfortably up through the limestone rock. Animal tracks or shortcuts can tempt you to stray from the path relatively easily in this section, but they all lead more or less clearly between two signs to the hilltop on the slope beyond which extends the valley pasture of **La Plana**, 1750m. In fact it is an enormous funnel-shaped hollow, overgrown with grass. There's a derelict hut on the left below and on the right a walled pool which serves as a trough for the grazing animals. A path leads to the east across some pastures (see Alternative), but take the direct and shorter ascent, almost in a straight line, which follows the broad limestone ridge ahead. Two very conspicuous acorn trees stand on the barren limestone slope and the left one serves as a point of orientation. Keeping heading towards this across the pastureland and you come to a large cairn where a path begins ascending northeastwards over limestone rock and through box trees. Cairns guide you along the way and most of them are clearly visible. As soon as the top of the tree comes into view you need to look out for a cairn on a boulder. The path forks here: straight on goes a short way to the east, then turns off diagonally left and passes the tree far over on the right outside the compact limestone rock; stay left on the ascending grassy path which a little later becomes a broad, almost six foot deep channel and climbs up past the tree a short distance away. As soon as the trig point on the summit is visible, head straight towards it and arrive at Castillo Mayor, 2015m, where a vast panorama awaits you.

26 To the spring and through the gorge of Río Yaga

A ramble through the landscape of gorges around Escuaín

Escuaín – Surgencia del Yaga – Barranco Garganta – Senda colgada – Escuaín

Location: Escalona, 600m.
Starting point: Escuaín, 1210m.
Walking times: Escuaín – Surgencia del Yaga ¾ hr.; Surgencia del Yaga – Barranco Garganta 1½ hrs.; Barranco Garganta – start of Senda colgada – ¾ hr. Senda colgada – Escuaín 2 hrs.; total time 5 hrs.
Difference in height: 340m.
Grade: steep ascent to the Yaga spring. For the walk through the Barranco del Yaga you require sure-footedness, some climbing ability and route-finding skills. Really steep path to the Senda Colgada.
Recommended map: Ordesa y Monte Perdido, 1:25,000 (Parques Nacionales de España 1); published by Ministerio de Fomento, 2000.
Stops and accommodation: bars and restaurants in Escalona.
Tip: the walk through the Barranco del Yaga is at its most beautiful when there is water in the gorge (pretty bathing pools), but it is still very attractive even if the streambed has dried up. If there is a lot of water you will have to cope with wet feet. If you want to avoid walking through the Barranco del Yaga, then the descent to Surgencia del Yaga is also a very worthwhile objective.

Well-devised, bold paths across the gorge wall, a spring waterfall in the midst of luxuriant vegetation, multi-coloured rock walls and fantastic pools, a fabulously shaped opening to the gorge – unusual and exciting impressions of nature together with changes in orientation are on the agenda for this round walk through and above the Barranco del Yaga.

Go past the church in **Escuaín** on the right and follow the idyllic village path in between natural stone walls. You quickly reach the inconspicuous streambed of Barranco Lugar where you cross over onto the other side and follow the path across old terraces. After the sign for Surgencia del Yaga you come to a second signpost with the same inscription where an indistinct grassy track joins from the left; this is the Senda Colgada which you will use for the return. Keep straight on and immediately the steep descent path starts to wind down across the slopes of the gorge. You need to be especially careful when you come to the natural stone steps because they are often really greasy, and therefore slippery.

Now and then the dense forest of box trees and oak trees allows you a view down into the deep Garganta de Escuaín with the turquoise pools and small ledges. Climb up some artificially laid rock steps to a small tunnel in the rock, and afterwards there's a broad wooden ladder across a broken-off section. Immediately afterwards a side path branches off right at a sign which says 'Bañarse prohibido' (no swimming) and you continue straight

ahead and a little later reach the bottom of the gorge. The widely fanned **Surgencia del Yaga**, 1060m, cascades down the rock opposite. (If you want to see the point at which the spring flows out of the rock and the exit of the of the famous cave system of Escuaín on the other side, scramble up the rock on the left of the waterfall. Go along the obvious forest path to the spring and further on to the cave exit.) Continue up the river. It's possible to walk along the flat rocky banks between the huge walls of the broad gorge without any difficulty, but further on you meet projections, ledges, waterfalls and large boulders which require some easy climbing or going round the side. It's fun looking for the most suitable way round and you will often find it

Río Yaga spring.

easier to make progress on the left-hand side of the Río Yaga.

As soon as the large cleft of the Barranco Garganta joining from the right comes into view, you need to look out for cairns on the right-hand bank. Following these, leave the Yaga gorge to make a detour along a small path to the opening of the Barranco Garganta hidden behind dense vegetation.

After a short while you come to some large boulders which you have to climb through; its best to keep as far as possible on the left of the streambed to find the easiest way to the 40m high steep cliff of the **Barranco Garganta**, 1150m, enclosed by a spectacular hallway of rocks – a gigantic masterpiece of erosion. Return to the Barranco del Yaga where flatter sections now alternate with some technically easy climbing through a labyrinth of rocks. Take a path round a very narrow section (cairns) which climbs up the slope on the right and leads back to the broad streambed beyond the narrowing rocks.

The gorge climb ends here and you leave the barranco at some cairns on the left-hand bank. An indistinct and at first really impassable path with small cairns goes up the steep slope and after ten minutes you meet a well-trodden cross path, the **Senda Colgada**, 1400m. Follow it to the left and walk along the shady ridge path above the gorge back to **Escuaín**.

Lushly green vegetation of the Río Yaga gorge.

27 Along the Camino de los Miradores

Marvellous path with views above the Garganta de Escuaín

Revilla – Miradores – Barranco de Angonés – Revilla

Location: Escalona, 600m.
Starting point: tight right-hand bend before Revilla, 1200m; park here or at the side of the road.
Walking times: car park – Miradores ½ hr.; Miradores – Barranco de Angonés ¾ hr.; Barranco de Angonés – Revilla ¾ hr., total time 2 hrs.
Difference in height: 200m.

Grade: easy walk on well-trodden paths. Sections, where the route is unclear, are marked with cairns. Mostly shady path.
Recommended map: Ordesa y Monte Perdido, 1:25,000 (Parques Nacionales de España 1); published by Ministerio de Fomento, 2000.
Stops and accommodation: bar and restaurant in Lamiana.

Several viewing balconies have been constructed not far from the half-abandoned hamlet of Revilla high above the Garganta de Escuaín which allow you the most beautiful views down into the gorge of the Río Yaga. A short detour on the return from this easy round walk leads to the Barranco de Angonés which, at this point, is at its most enchanting with an almost perfect interplay of rock, water and light.

The path turns off left directly on the bend before **Revilla**, keeps to the foot of a rock face and after a few minutes reaches the little bridge over the Barranco Consusa. Walk beside the cleft of the gorge on the other side for a bit, then turn off and walk along the rock face towards an overgrown rock tower. There the path swings onto the broad wooded and terrace on the slope high above the Río Yaga. Flat areas alternate with gentle inclines and soon you reach the first walled *mirador* with an open view of the steep rock walls of the gorge to which there are clinging all sorts of trees and bushes, and emerald green pools and troughs lie sparkling in the depths below. Escuaín lies hidden on the rock spur opposite, surrounded by beautiful terraced slopes.

Continue along the path and one hundred metres after a large boulder on the left-hand side of the path, the path forks and you keep straight ahead (take the right-hand ascending path on the return) and quickly arrive at the two **miradores**, 1250m. The Mirador de Sacos lies on the right of the path high above the Barranco de Angonés, and a few minutes afterwards the path ends at the Mirador de Gratarella, which sits enthroned like an eagle's nest on a narrow ledge of rock above the Garganta de Escuaín and allows you fabulous views into the gorge.

The return first leads you back to the fork mentioned earlier. Turn off left here and climb up through dense wood to a higher plateau on which the path becomes flatter again and now runs through stunted vegetation. On your left-hand side you soon see some pastureland that has a long natural stone wall as its boundary. Follow the numerous cairns across the rocky ground as far as a broad cross path which you take to the left.

The path runs along the wall, then through forest and past a National Park information board and sign. Slowly you come closer to the *barranco*, pass an overhanging rock and reach soon after that the bridge across the **Barranco de Angonés**, 1400m. The smoothly polished rock pools and the water-falls of the *barranco* and the im-

Barranco de Angonés.

pressive surroundings of the gorge invite you to stop for a rest.

On the return, first walk back to the long stone wall, keep straight on there along the path and to another bridge across the *barranco*. Cross over the streambed and shortly afterwards the path goes briefly over rocky ground where cairns help you find the way. After a stretch of flat ground you begin to go gently downhill as Revilla comes into view. Past a strikingly huge boulder the path goes round a sharp bend and runs towards the village. In front of the church turn off left and then immediately take the next turn-off to the right. Go directly along the village path through **Revilla** and to the road which leads you back to the starting point.

28 Circo de Gurrundué, 1980m

Wonderful mountain walk to a huge high mountain basin

Revilla – Barranco de Angonés – Barranco Garganta – Circo de Gurrundué and back

Location: Escalona, 600m.
Starting point: tight right-hand bend before Revilla, 1200m; park here or at the side of the road.
Walking times: Revilla – Barranco de Angonés 1 hr.; Barranco de Angonés – Barranco Garganta 1 hr.; Barranco Garganta – Circo de Gurrandué 1 hr.; return 2½ hrs.; total time 5½ hrs.
Difference in height: 780m.
Grade: long, but technically not a very

demanding walk on mostly obvious paths, only without paths in the last section where there are no serious route-finding problems.
Cairns. Often shady.
Recommended map: Ordesa y Monte Perdido, 1:25,000 (Parques Nacionales de España 1); published by Ministerio de Fomento, 2000.
Stops and accommodation: bar and restaurant in Lamiana.

Only a few walkers manage to reach the large mountain basin where the Río Yaga has its source. The wild and barren landscape of the rock basin formed by the glaciers contrasts impressively with the green pastureland and the range of soft hills on the other side of the Río Yaga gorge. This enormous amphitheatre is of exceptional beauty and even the walk there through this isolated region of the National Park provides you with a superb experience.

From the car park walk along the road to **Revilla**, go through the village, past the church and up left to the path which leads away from the village and then changes direction round a conspicuously sharp bend. On a gradual incline walk past a subsidiary path (Consusa superior), then across heavily eroded rocky slopes marked with cairns until you come to a little bridge across the Barranco Consusa. Cross over the streambed and soon reach some enclosed pastures. Ignore cairns which lead to the left and follow the path straight on beside the natural stone wall behind which you enter a dense mixed forest of yew, acorn, hazelnut, holly and ash. After you have passed the National Park boundary the path soon brings you closer to the **Barranco de Angonés**, 1400m. Cross the terrifyingly steep-sided streambed on

Circo de Gurundué
Refugio de Foratarruego
1980

Circo de Gurrundué.

the bridge and immediately afterwards the path divides and you keep right in the direction of Forratarruego/Puerto de Revilla. A strenuous climb up the hillside brings you to a terrace covered with pines, box trees and gorse across which the path now runs more on the level until it swings into the gorge of the **Barranco Garganta**, 1600m, and crosses the streambed. On the other side of the *barranco* you meet a signposted fork where the path goes left to a lower level of the Circo de Gurrandué.

Go right in the direction of Puerto de Revilla/Gurrandué and now you have a steep slope ahead, 150 vertical metres of climbing, after which you come to a pretty little clearing. The path continues diagonally to the right through the wood with the gradient easing off noticeably. The vegetation gradually thins out and across grassy slopes you head towards a conspicuous limestone wall which extends north-westwards. The path is really indistinct at times and crossing the slopes diagonally, make for the end of the rock wall where you will soon clearly see the Refugio de Foratarruego.

Beyond the rock wall you climb the slope up to the height of the Refugio (sturdy self-catering hut for 4-6 people) and then walk over to the edge of the enormous **Circo de Gurrandué**, 1980m.

29 A round walk from Tella

History combined with a vast panorama

Dolmen and Ermitas of Tella

Location: Escalona, 600m.
Starting point: Tella, 1335m. Car park at the entrance to the village.
Walking times: total time for the round walk, 1 hr.
Difference in height: 65m.
Grade: stroll along a good path.
Recommended map: Ordesa y Monte Perdido, 1:25,000 (Parques Nacionales de España 1); published by Ministerio de Fomento, 2000.
Stops and accommodation: bar and restaurant in Escalona and Hospital de Tella.
Tip: the dolmen of Tella, also called Piedra del Vasar o Losa de la Campa, lies on the left of the road a good kilometre before the village. A sign indicates the site. It dates from the Neolithic period and was not excavated until 1954.

The good 1300m high mountain hamlet of Tella is a natural look-out post with an unusual collection of cultural sights. In the surrounding area of this pretty village you can not only visit the famous dolmen of Tella, but also three Ermitas, the oldest of which dates from the 11th century. They are linked by a comfortable round walk from Tella and offers you a 360° panorama.

Pick up the round path at the village church in **Tella**, walk through this pretty village, past the village well, as far as the last house where the village road ends. This is where the pilgrims' path begins across the enclosed meadow slopes to your first objective, the 16th century Ermita de Fajanillas. The hermitage is easy to spot with its compact tower. Keep right at the first fork and go left at the next and after a few minutes go right at another fork up to the Ermita with the walled forecourt. From here you can see the Ermita Virgen de la Peña, also built in the 16th century, and an obvious path goes quickly up to this beautiful viewing point.

Your next objective, the Ermita de los Santos San Juan y Pablo, nestles in the shelter of the fissured crag which dominates the view westwards into the valley of the Río Yaga. Go back down the path again and a few metres before the first hermitage take the path turning off left. It runs swiftly downhill

The Ermita San uan y Pablo nestling at the foot of the Puntón de las Brujas.

and at the height of the Ermita a small path turns off left and leads to a secluded little spot in the shade of the Puntón de las Brujas. The Ermita de los Santos San Juan y Pablo dates from the 11th century and is supposed to be the oldest maintained building in the whole of the Sobrarbe region. Continue your round walk along the path through a shady pinewood, come past an information board and you are walking again in the direction of the village. There's a short stretch along broad sloping firebreaks following some cairns, and then the path leads back to the church at the entrance to the village.

olmen of Tella.

30 Faja de la Tormosa, 1960m

Enchanting mountain path into the Circo de Pineta

Refugio de Pineta – Faja de la Tormosa – Cascada de Marboré – Refugio de Pineta

Location: Bielsa, 1020m.
Starting point: Refugio de Pineta, 1240m; a good 2km before the Parador de Bielsa on the left below the road (signposted).
Walking times: Refugio de Pineta – climb up to Faja de la Tormosa 2 hrs.; Faja de la Tormosa – Cascada de Marboré 2 hrs.; return 1½ hrs.; total time 5½ hrs.
Difference in height: 720m.
Grade: long and demanding walk with a very steep ascent up to the *faja*; before the Cascada de Marboré short climbing section (I) with chain. GR path (marked red and white) as far as the *faja*, after that good paths; cairns.
Shady only as far as the *faja*. Be careful in rain, snow and ice when the walk is very dangerous.
Recommended map: Ordesa y Monte Perdido, 1:25,000 (Parques Nacionales de España 1); published by Ministerio de Fomento, 2000.
Stops and accommodation: Refugio de Pineta (with a warden all year round) and Parador de Bielsa at th end of the valley road.
Tips: the walk in the direction given is less strenuous than the other way round because you have to negotiate the steep gradient between the valley and the *faja* at the start and the descent in the Circo de Pineta is less hard work, added to which, the views are decidedly better.
Alternative: Collado de Añisclo, 2450m: spectacular pass between Valle de Pineta and Cañón de Añisclo, surrounded by the huge rock masses of Punta de las Olas on the right, La Tuca on the left, and with a fantastic view. At the junction to the Faja de la Tormosa the red and white marked GR path keeps left and goes up the grassy slope round narrow zigzags. The rocky ground and areas of scree broaden out with increasing height and sometimes the very steep gradient becomes really exhausting. Cairns lead you across to the slope of the Collado, where you continue over rock steps and ledges. Then the path runs up to the col which, on the south side, drops down into the broad green Añisclo valley.
Very demanding walk in high-alpine terrain at a high altitude (1210m) and with exceedingly steep ascents. Be careful on the descent on the steep scree slope! There and back from the fork, 2½ hrs.

The Faja de la Tormosa runs horizontally across the north facing walls of the Pineta valley. On the green mountain path lined with countless flowers, a fabulous view opens out of the huge basin-shaped valley of Valle de Pineta, the precipitous crags between Pico de Pineta and La Munia and the gentle high pastures of la Larri. The dramatic Cascada del Cinca is a magnificent end to an adventurous day's hike.

From the **Refugio de Pineta**, walk straight to the streambed of the Río Cinca. There's a cairn at the point where you can cross over onto the other bank and you will see another cairn and the obvious path leading into the wood. After going across a meadow the path begins to climb towards a rock face and turns off to the right. The steep ascent up through the wood begins immediately past a National Park sign. Further up the wood thins out, the path becomes flatter and you walk towards the Barranco Castiecho and cross the streambed keeping an eye on the cairns. The path immediately steepens up again, first keeping through beech and birch trees, then briefly across an open steep slope.

Now there's a lengthy section of very strenuous gradient where, now and again, a bit of climbing is necessary up rock ledges. The gruelling ascent only eases off a little when you reach open ground. Then the path steepens up again and winds its way up the slope to a fork with signposts at the climb up to the **Faja de las Tormosa**, 1960m. Left goes up to the Collado de Añisclo (see 'Alternative'). Follow the path straight on which descends gently at first and then later runs on the level, over the grassy slopes strewn with rocks.

The path brings you closer to the Barranco Tormosa, dominated by steep rock walls, and you cross the stream below a cascade. The path gently rises again on the other side across a grassy plateau, then gradually goes across broad meadow slopes to the Barranco Tubo, beyond which you soon reach the streambed of another *barranco*. The heavily distorted and parallel layered rock faces in the surrounding area make a striking backdrop. You now cross several stream channels in close succession and on the way you come past a small rock spring on the left-hand side of the path. The view

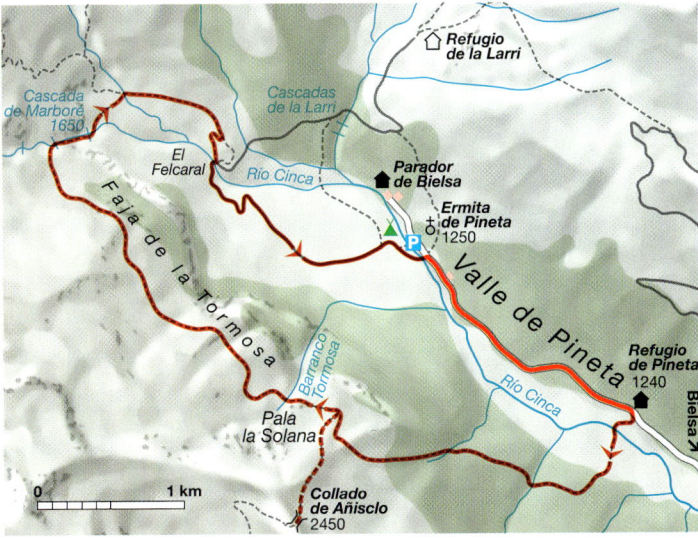

Several times cascades stop the faja path.

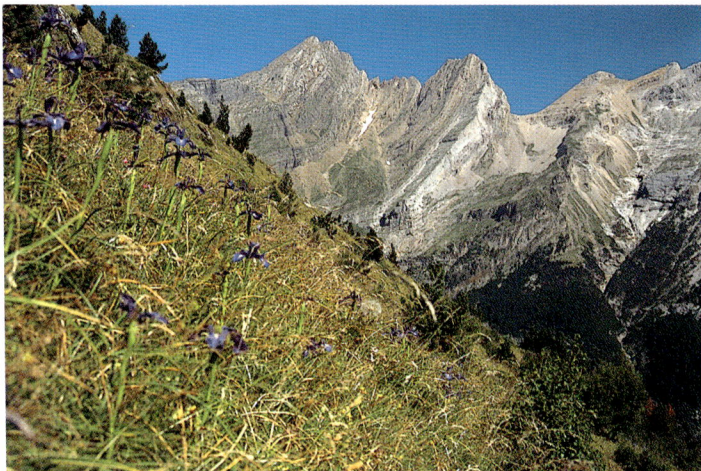

Countless lilies adorn the faja path..

over to the other side of the valley is awesome: the high pastures of la Larri with the meandering river, dominated by the backdrop of peaks of the mountains along the border which culminate over to the east in the mighty Pico de la Munia.

After a short rise the path keeps on the level and runs across steeply falling slopes, then the grand Circo de Pineta comes into view behind a protruding precipice with countless cascades. The twisting descent into the valley begins straight away and you cross over a cleft of the gorge following cairns Continue descending a rock spur and after that there's an easy climb down a sheer drop (chain) and then the path swiftly leads down to the bridge at the foot of the thundering **Cascada de Marboré**, 1650m. The path keeps close to the gorge for a short way on the other bank, then moves away from it and forks. Take the right fork in the direction of the valley, first descending through high ferns, then later through a wood until you come to a roadway. Continue along to the right and cross the wild valley stream on the bridge. The roadway then brings you to the road which leads back to the **Refugio de Pineta**.

31 Llanos y Cascadas de la Larri, 1620m

Waterfalls, meadows and majestic mountain backdrops

Ermita de Pineta – Llanos de la Larri – Cascadas de la Larri – Ermita de Pineta

Location: Bielsa, 1020m.
Starting point: Ermita de Pineta, 1250m, just before the Parador de Bielsa.
Walking times: Ermita de Pineta – Salto de la Larri 1¼ hrs.; return across the Cascadas 1¼ hrs.; total time 2½ hrs.
Difference in height: 370m.
Grade: easy round walk on good paths;

GR path in the first part (marked red and white). Hefty incline between Ermita and den Llanos.
Recommended map: Ordesa y Monte Perdido, 1:25.000 (Parques Nacionales de España 1); published by Ministerio de Fomento, 2000.
Accommodation: Parador de Bielsa.

The rock masses tower up in the Circo de Pinetal like reminders of geological upthrusts and appear to totally cut off the valley. On la Larri plateau (from 'larrea', the Basque for meadow) the magnificent view extends round the mighty peaks of the Marboré massif and the Sierra de la Suca. The walk through the former glacial valley with meadows full of flowers, green pastures and cascades is a special treat in early summer when the peaks and the steep walls of the Pineta are still covered in snow.

At the forecourt of the **Ermita de Pineta**, take the signposted GR path to Llanos de la Larri/Pico de la Munia. The broad path leads you into a fairytale beech wood and in the shade of these gigantic trees, ascend steeply uphill for half an hour to a roadway which is the start of some unwooded pastureland. Waymarkers and cairns now lead you straight up along a cross path which takes a shortcut across the long bends of the roadway. Just before the plateau you join the roadway which you follow and before long reach the **Llanos de la Larri**, 1580m. The roadway suddenly stops here and there's an obvious path sometimes deeply furrowed, which you follow past the

The Llanos de la Larri are dominated by the Monte Perdido massif.

Refugio de la Larri (self-catering hut for 4 people), a short distance away on the right, and through the vast high pasture you head towards the large waterfall which plunges down at the end of the valley between narrow rock faces. You now reach the turn-round point of your walk, the **Salto de la Larri**, 1620m, with beautiful pools inviting you to take a cool, refreshing swim.

Now begin your return back along the same path to the point where you met the roadway for the first time on the way up. Follow the roadway right, go through a large gate and come to the bridge over the Río de la Larri which flows down a beautiful series of cascades over the red-coloured rock. A few paces further on the signposted path turns off left to the **Cascadas**, 1500m. Quickly descend through a shady mixed wood along the well-stabilised path into the valley and on the way, there are viewing balconies from where you can see the magnificent rock and its thundering waterfalls. After the terrain has levelled out, you come to the signpost for Cascadas de la Larri/Puente de la Larri. Keep along the broad path here on the right of the stream as far as the roadway and the bridge over the Río Cinca. Then it's another few paces left along the road back to the **Ermita de Pineta**.

32 Balcón de Pineta, 2500m, and Lago de Marboré, 2595m

Spectacular climb through the Circo de Pineta to the glacier slopes of Monte Perdido

Parador de Bielsa – Balcón de Pineta – Lago de Marboré and back

Location: Bielsa, 1020m.
Starting point: car park at the free camping ground near the Parador de Bielsa, 1300m; about 300m before the Parador there's a roadway branching off left onto the other bank of the Río Cinca.
Walking times: car park – Balcón de Pineta 4 hrs.; Balcón de Pineta – Lago de Marboré ½ hr.; return 3¾ hrs.; total time 8¼ hrs.
Difference in height: 1295m.

Grade: long and very strenuous walk on good paths. A big variation in height and a continuously steep ascent up the whole of the Circo de Pineta. Practically no shade.
Recommended map: Ordesa y Monte Perdido, 1:25,000 (Parques Nacionales de España 1); published by Ministerio de Fomento, 2000.
Stops and accommodation: bar and restaurant in the Parador de Bielsa; bar at the campsite (only in summer).

Furrowed glacial slopes, misshapen piles of rock, bizarre peak formations, precipitous rock spikes, thundering waterfalls – the dramatic forces of nature are ever-present on your ascent up to the Balcón de Pineta. The long and exhausting walk up through the Circo de Pineta to the wide high plateau at the foot of the Marboré peak is rewarded with magnificent views of the mountains and striking contrasts in scenery.

At the **car park** follow the roadway through the campground and walk towards the end of the valley to the bridge across the Río Cinca gorge. Straight after the bridge the signposted path to Marboré/Picos de Astazu begins on the left to the Balcón de Pineta. The gradient immediately

increases and at first the path goes beside the stream, then moves away from it at a yellow arrow, levels out and stays for a longish stretch through high, dense ferns with only a slight incline. The large cascade in the basin-shaped valley is always in sight. Gradually the path begins to ascend, at first still winding its way through ferns then going across open ground and heading for the steep wall of the Circo. After you have passed a spring with a walled container, there's a fork. The path to the left leads to the Faja Tormosa (see Walk 30) and to the Collado de Añisclo, but you keep right and now begin the actual ascent through the Circo de Pineta. The stony path skilfully uses the ledges, projections and terraces in the superb semi-circle, while the gradient steadily increases. After crossing the slope the path runs up again round a succession of bends through the steep head of the valley. Gradually the curved rock parapet comes into view which cuts off the western slope. Further up the path keeps heading for the rock wall, turns left there and climbs up parallel to it. After an alleyway through the rock you reach the fabulous **Balcón de Pineta**, 2500m. You are rewarded here with breath-taking views after the exhausting ascent. Continue past the wrought-iron, cross along the obvious path north-westwards, cross over fields of moraine and end up at the **Lago de Marboré**, 2595m. In the rock wall on the opposite bank, the narrow notch with the Refugio de Tucarroya (bivouac shed) is clearly visible. Cross through the gap into the neighbouring French Cirque d'Estaubé.

The Perdido glacier.

33 Lagos de La Munia, 2510m

To the two mountain lakes in the earliest mountains of the Pyrenees

Borda Brunet – Lagos de La Munia and back

Location: Bielsa, 1020m.
Starting point: car park at the Borda Brunet, 1680m, in the Valle Río Real, about 5km along the track beyond Chisagües. After Chisagües turn off left just behind the petrol station at Parzán. About a 20 mins. drive along the track.
Walking times: car park – Lagos de La Munia 2½ hrs.; return 2 hrs.; total time 4½ hrs.
Difference in height: 830m.
Grade: moderately difficult walk along a track and marked paths with some steeper sections in between. No shade at all along the way.
Recommended map: Ordesa y Monte Perdido, 1:25,000 (Parques Nacionales de España 1); published by Ministerio de Fomento, 2000.
Stops and accommodation: bar at the petrol station at Parzán.
Alternative: Collado de La Munia, 2850m: marvellous view of the Cirque de Troumousse, Pico de La Munia, Robiñera and Marboré peak. The path to the Collado runs along the right-hand bank of the first lake, at the end ascends up to the higher platform on the slope where the second lake is situated and keeps to the right-hand side there too. Then the path branches off diagonally right, soon heads to the north again towards the obvious col along which runs the western ridge of La Munia. Keep left at a waymarked junction

along the way – a path to the right leads up to the Collado Robiñera in the east – and then climb steeply up the slope towards the Collado where there are cairns as well as white and red waymarkers to guide you. The gradient increases at the end and zigzags up the steep slope over scree to the Collado de La Munia. There and back 1¾ hrs. from Lagos.
Collado Las Coronetas, 2160m: very beautiful viewing point over the Circo de Pineta, Collado Añisclo, Tres Sorores and the whole range of mountains of the Valle de Pineta. Just before the sharp bend in the forest track you turn off left at the signpost for Pineta along the GR11, cross over the stream and on the other side follow the red and white marked path across pastures strewn with large boulders. Soon after you have crossed the Barranco de las Coronetas the path ascends the steep eroded slope on the right of the *barranco*, goes briefly across a stabilised section of path, goes through a hollow after that and then, maintaining its height, runs along the streambed. After a gentle ascent up a slope it reaches the Collado below which there's a marvellous plateau of pastureland.
If you walk a little further over the col to the foot of the Tozal de las Coronetas, you are afforded a more extensive panorama. There and back 2 hrs. from the signpost.

A sharp contrast of colour and shape characterises the mountains surrounding the Lagos de La Munia: the light grey polished Peña Blanca and just to the side of it, the reddish brown rock of the enormous craggy rock of La Munia. The enthralling landscape in the Circo de La Munia with the two lakes is part of the area of the original mountain mass of the Pyrenees which is made up of crystalline rock.
Your walk begins at the **car park** at the **Borda Brunet** at first along the track

that you follow up the valley for about two kilometres. On some flat pastureland the GR leaves the track to the left at a signpost (see Aternative to Collado de las Coronetas), but you walk a few paces further on and turn off left from the track just after the sharp hairpin bend at the cairn. Go uphill along the eroded path, keep left at the following junction and climb up the small rise behind which the path now runs on the level towards the

One of the Lagos de La Munia.

Barranco del Clot de los Gabachos. Cross over the streambed, climb steeply up a rocky knoll, then the path loses height again and heads towards the Barranco Pietramula to then turn northwards and ascend the pasture slopes. At first gradually, then on a steeper incline you come closer to the edge of the Barranco del Clot de los Gabachos and walk parallel to it further up the grassy slopes which gradually become rocky terrain. You come past a conspicuous boulder with an arrow and La Munia marked in red and the now flatter path proceeds across the steep valley slope covered in debris with cairns keeping you to the route. The col, behind which lie the

lakes, comes into view after a small projection on the slope. The path runs downhill into the the streambed, heads towards the col and reaches the first of the **Lagos de La Munia**, 2510m, with a rocky island.

The path to the second lake stays clearly on the right-hand bank, climbs up the small ledge on the slope at the end and comes to the lake behind it. A superb viewing point can be reached in a quarter of an hour if you turn off left before the first lake and follow the outflow stream to the west as far as the edge of the steep cliffs.

34 Over the Puerto de Barrosa, 2535m, to the Lacs de Barroude, 2355m

Mule path onto a high border pass with a delightful detour to the lakes

Hospital de Parzán – Cabaña de Barrosa – Puerto de Barrosa – Lacs de Barroude and back

Location: Bielsa, 1020m.
Starting point: forest track into the Barrosa valley, 1400m, just before the bridge across the Río Barrosa. Car park at the start of the track.
Walking times: car park – Cabaña de Barrosa 1¼ hrs.; Cabaña de Barrosa – Puerto de Barrosa 1¾ hrs.; Puerto de Barrosa – Lacs de Barrosa ½ hr.; return 3¼ hrs.; total time 6¾ hrs.
Difference in height: 1315m (including return ascent from the Lacs de Barroude to the Puerto de Barrosa).

Grade: technically easy, but long walk with a large variation in height on predominantly good paths; generally only a moderately steep walk, except on the climb to the Puerto which is hard-going. The whole walk is virtually without any shade.
Recommended map: Bielsa-Val de Chistau, 1:40,000; published by Editorial Pirineo, 1998.
Stops and accommodation: bar and restaurant at the petrol station at Parzán; Refuge de Barroude (staffed in summer).

The huge rock masses of Pico Robiñera and La Munia close off the broad valley of the Río Barrosa in the west. Through the less precipitous north-facing end of the valley on the other hand you can walk along a pleasant path over the pass onto the Puerto de Barrosa where the view is dominated by the elongated Murailles de Barroude. The Lacs de Barroude lie in a pretty morainal landscape at the foot of the five hundred metre towering sheer rock face.

At the car park take the **forest track** and ascend up through a wood, past a sharp right-hand turn-off, and immediately afterwards the track swings northwards and then slowly bends round into the valley of the Río Barrosa. There are pretty terraces up on the slope on the right of the path, and the remains of an old cable railway on the left which once used to transport lead and silver from the mountain of the Sierra de Liena. The stony path doesn't level out until you reach the height of the stream and soon you cross over a covered water channel beyond which the path now continues gently up and down close to the stream where there are lots of little islands of brightly coloured flowers. Meadow grass, pine trees and large boulders characterise the scene until your path, marked with cairns, leads through several side branches (dried up in summer) of the Río Barrosa and meets the main stream. Only just before the Cabaña de Barrosa which has been visible for some time, does the path change onto the opposite bank, and then it climbs up the hillside and heads towards the hut. Behind the **Cabaña de Barrosa** (emergency shelter), 1760m, the path now starts to ascend the

pasture slopes round long bends, comes past a walled animal pen in the shelter of a large boulder and zigzags easily uphill in a north-easterly direction easily. Then it crosses the grassy slopes northwards and goes round the steep crag which is cut through by the Barranco de las Neveras. Another change in direction of the path to the east is followed by a sharp hairpin bend to which is joined a long north-westerly diagonal across the slopes. It leads you uphill over to the slope of the pass and even if it isn't steep, it requires a last burst of energy. Narrow bends take you first up the rise of the col, rather bleak and covered in fragments of stone, then round wider bends until it reaches the broad **Puerto de Barrosa**, 2535m. Here you follow the signpost to the Barroude lakes and descend the col down the zigzag path. The large lake with its small rocky island quickly comes into view and after crossing a slope the path brings you closer to the **Lac de Barroude**, 2355m, and then runs on the right of it towards a small hill with the Refuge de Barroude. Directly next to the hut lies the smaller of the two lakes in a hollow.

Puerto de Barrosa.

35 Valle de Chistau

Pretty villages and scenery around Gistaín

Plan – Gistaín – Serveto – Collado de Peña de Artiés – Plan

Location: Plan, 1120m.
Starting point: Plan, tourist office.
Walking times: Plan – Serveto 2¼ hrs.; Serveto – Collado de Peña de Artiés ½ hr.; Collado Peña de Artiés – Plan 1½ hrs.; total time 4¼ hrs.
Difference in height: 300m; negligible gradients.
Grade: easy round walk on GR and PR

paths (marked red and white or yellow and white).
Steep incline from Plan to Gistaín, however.
Recommended map: Bielsa-Val de Chistau, 1:40,000; published by Editorial Pirineo, 1998.
Stops and accommodation: bars and restaurants in Plan and Gistaín.

The wild Río Cinqueta valley was for a long time one of the most closed-off valleys in the Aragon Pyrenees. This contributed to the preservation of the local dialect and the continuation of traditional customs. Together with the villages where the village centre retains much of its original character, the great charm of the Valle de Chistén (as it's called there) on this round walk is shown to its full advantage.

The round walk begins at the little wooden hut of the **tourist information** along the road to San Juan de Plan and Gistaín. Go past a bar and turn immediately left onto the steep village road. It takes you through the village up to the washing well where the waymarked PR path to Gistaín begins. This shady path ascends steadily across terraced slopes and after just under half an hour the first houses of the village come into view. Cross over a roadway, meet it once more a little later on and follow it now to **Gistaín**, 1420m. Keep heading for the huge peel-tower, walk past it on the right and along the ascending narrow street to the church. Continue there along the village path uphill which straight-away turns round the corner and comes to a washing place where the signposted GR path to Serveto starts. It runs across the steep terraces of Gistaín, meets a track which you take to the left, but leave again on the left after a few minutes at a wooden post waymarker. The path now leads on the level and you keep straight ahead at a fork. After a longish stretch the path gently descends and several scattered

Serveto.

huts appear on the cultivated slopes at the foot of Peña de San Martín. A PR alternative descends left to Plan, but you stay on the GR path and soon reach a roadway. Go left here.

Now walk along the edge of a broad high valley with green cattle pastures and numerous barns which show signs of intensive agriculture. After you have crossed a ford of the Barranco Salina the roadway goes round a right-hand bend and immediately afterwards your path branches off left and leads leisurely down through box trees and little walls into the valley basin. Keep left at a junction and arrive in **Serveto**, 1320m. Leave the village again behind the church and you come straightaway to the signpost for Plan por el Collet Peña Artiés. From now on you are now walking along the PR path again, at first down to the little bridge across the stream, then along the roadway as far as the three-pronged junction where your path continues in the middle of the dividing roadways. Up a gentle incline and after a few bends you come onto the **Collado de Peña de Artiés**, 1360m. If you are still feeling energetic enough you can make a detour onto the top of the Peña de Artiés to enjoy the beautiful views from there.

The return to Plan is along a panoramic path at the foot of the vertical rock faces of Peña de San Martín, 200m above the valley floor. First of all walk directly along the top of the steep rock, then later across the lower slopes of this impressive rock tower, cross two steep *barrancos*, then gradually descend into the valley. At a barn take a shortcut from a roadway then meet it again a few metres below and follow it to the valley road. Go about 70m to the right and the path leads onto the meadows of the Río Cinqueta where you walk back to Plan on the left-hand bank of the main course of the river. At some farm buildings you meet a track where you go left to return to your starting point at the edge of **Plan**.

36 Ibón de Plan (Basa de la Mora), 1910m

A fairytale lake in front of a bizarre backdrop

Saravillo – Las Solanas – Refugio de Labasar – Ibón de Plan and back

Location: Plan, 1120m.
Starting point: village square of Saravillo, 1010m.
Walking times: Saravillo – Las Solanas 1½ hrs.; Las Solanas – Refugio de Labasar 1¼ hrs. Refugio de Labasar – Ibón de Plan ½ hr., return 2½ hrs.; total time 5¾ hrs.
Difference in height: 915m.

Grade: not a difficult walk along GR path (marked red and white) with some steep inclines. Mostly in forest shade.
Recommended map: Bielsa-Val de Chistau, 1:40,000; published by Editorial Pirineo, 1998.
Stops and accommodation: bar in Saravillo, bar and restaurant at Los Vives campsite.

The inhabitants of the valley also call the Ibón de Plan, Basa de la Mora (lake of the Moorish woman). According to legend, lying buried in the lake is a beautiful Moorish princess who lost her way in the mountains before the wars between the Moors and the Christians. Irrespective of the legend, the lake, surrounded by the bizarre pre-summits of Cotiella, is one of the most beautiful mountain lakes which makes it an excellent objective for an excursion. Many drive there by car up along the long track to the Refugio de Labasar from where the lake can be reached in about half an hour's stroll. However, the delightfully scenic hiking trail through quiet woods is more enjoyable.

The Ibón de Plan.

The **village square of Saravillo** lies somewhat hidden in the eastern part of the village (if in doubt, ask for the 'plaza mayor'). There's a signpost for the GR 15. Ibón/Ref. de Armeña on the front of a house and you go through the narrow street in the direction indicated, and beyond the houses you come to another signpost, this time for Basa de la Mora/Barbaruens. Your path soon becomes a track and after about 100m take the path to the right at a waymarked wooden post, cross over a covered water channel further on and join the track once more. Directly opposite there's a shortcut (cairn) along a scree path which again, soon meets the track. Continue to follow the sign for the Basa de la Mora/Barbaruens. After a clearing in the wood, you walk high above the Río Cinqueta valley for a while, with fine views of the splendid coloured steep walls. Then the path turns into the Barranco Gallinés (at a turn-off ascending up into the forest on the right) and you come to the streambed. It now continues on the other side up a steep incline and runs across wooded slopes with small clearings. You gain height quickly and come to a place called **La Solana**, 1470m, with springs and a retaining pool which you pass on the left as you continue the climb. The wooded slopes ease off a little and you keep straight ahead at a junction and meet the track. Here a little to the left, then, immediately after the right-hand bend at the cairns and waymarkings on the tree, go right again, onto the hiking trail and up the slope through the wood. You soon return to the track and follow it uphill as far as the sharp left-hand bend after your path once more leaves the track at the red and white cairn. After you have crossed the track again the path gets lost on the meadow slope and you follow the waymarkings on trees and stones along some indistinct tracks up to the **Refugio de Labasar**, 1925m. (Self catering hut, space for 6 people.) Take the path here starting at the Barbaruens signpost and first walk gradually downhill through rocky terrain, go through a wooden gate and reach the **Ibón de Plan**, 1910m, along the path across the meadow.

37 Walk round the Peña de la Una, 2550m

Through isolated and dramatic rocky debris in the Cotiella massif

Refugio de Labasar – Ibón de Plan – Collado de la Ribereta – Refugio de Labasar

Location: Plan, 1120m.

Starting point: Refugio de Labasar, 1925m, at the end of the 13km long roadway from Saravillo. Drive through the village on the asphalt road and take the track adjoining it which then divides several times on the way. Ignore the first fork in the direction of San Miguel and keep straight on at the second fork towards Labasar. Drive along the track takes about 40 mins.

Walking times: Refugio de Labasar – Ibón de Plan ½ hr.; Ibón de Plan – Collado de la Ribereta 2 ½ hrs.; Collado de la Ribereta – Refugio de Labasar 2 hrs.; total time 5 hrs.

Difference in height: 620m.

Grade: strenuous walk with steep to very steep sections (especially on the ascent of the channel to Valle de la Ribereta), frequently on scree covered terrain; incomplete cairns, sometimes without paths; route-finding needed on the climb up to the Collado. Sure-footedness and a good sense of direction essential. It is advisable not to go on the walk if there is fog.

Recommended map: Bielsa-Val de Chistau, 1:40,000; published by Editorial Pirineo, 1998.

Stops and accommodation: bar in Saravillo; bar and restaurant at Los Vives campsite.

Extreme contrasts in the landscape characterise this walk round the Peña de la Una in the northern massif of the Cotiella. The delightful scenery of lakes around the Ibón de Plan forms the prelude for a unique walk where elemental rock-forms are displayed in amazing diversity. Eroded mountain chains, wide valleys of scree, elegantly sweeping rock layers, strangely shaped flanks, aesthetically structured rock faces and geometrically perfect circles of scree – a beautiful and dramatic rock performance where solitude is the sole companion of the mountain walker.

On the Collado de la Ribereta.

At the **Refugio de Labasar** (self-catering hut, room for 6 people) follow the Barbaruens signpost. The red and white GR first runs a little way downhill and then through a delightful high plain with meadows, wooded hills, islands of rock and streams.

Cross over the streambed of the Barranco del Ibón, go through a thin pine wood and come to a marshy meadow which you cross along the obvious path and straight after that you find yourself at the **Ibón de Plan**, 1910m, which is also called Basa de la Mora based on a legend. Continue the path on the west side of the lake across the sloping wooded bank and head for the broad scree slope which drops down to the lake from the foot of the long rock wall. The dark coloured mark of a waterfall stands out on the steep rock face.

First a scree track, marked clearly with cairns, makes straight for the rock face, then turns off sharply to the right, crosses the scree slope parallel to it and heads towards a broad steep channel in the rock. The gradient quickly increases and becomes really steep as you follow the scree tracks uphill along the channel. A rock projection further up divides it into two and you take the broader branch of the channel here on the right. Immediately after

Agujas de Labasar.

going round the rock projection, leave the channel to the left (cairns mark the ascent). You are now standing in the Ribereta valley where you first ascend up across the grass, then over scree slopes on the right-hand side of the valley until you come to a small valley threshold beyond which emerges an undulating depression with numerous craters. The steeply sloping Cresta de Armeña now stretches out ahead, protecting the high valley to the south east.

Cross this along beside the cairns, and from time to time there are also some clear tracks visible and you head for the long gravel valley which runs south-westwards up along the foot of the Cresta de Armeña. The waymarkings now become sparser or are indeed missing altogether, some of them having been destroyed by scree slides and avalanches. After you have crossed over a snowfield which usually stays here, even in summer, keep in the bottom of the scree valley and ascend for some time up to an obvious scree path which crosses the slope to the right and heads towards the broad rock base of the Collado. As soon as you have reached the rock ledges, climb the rocky slope directly up to the **Collado de la Ribereta**,

A bizarre lump of rock – Peña de la Una.

2550m. An enormous limestone field stretches out in front of you which is furrowed with channels and gullies. This is divided into two valleys by the long ridge that extends down as far as the splintered rock needles of the Agujas de Labasar.

Your descent runs down through the right-hand valley below the Peña de la Una. Numerous cairns mark the route, at first leading you across small ledges on the slope, then down the left-hand side of the slope and eventually staying in the gully with a moderate up-and-down until you come to the tiny lake at the foot of the Agujas de Labasar. Go past the lake on the right and the path turns off shortly afterwards to the right and leads into the broad valley between the Punta es Litás and Pico Labasar.

The gradient becomes noticeably less steep, the stony valley becomes greener and the path now goes through a thin stand of pines to an old track which you follow to the right. This brings you to the roadway from Saravillo where you again turn right.

Before the bends you can take a shortcut over the meadow slopes up to the starting point at the **Refugio de Labasar**.

38 Ibón de Ordizeto, 2370m

The magnificent mountains around Valle de Gistaín

Pista de Lisier – Refugio de Lisier – Es Montarruego – Ibón de Ordizeto and back

Location: Plan, 1120m.
Starting point: Pista de Lisier, 1540m; a roadway branches off left from the forest track to Viadós, about 7.5km after the start of the track. Park at the junction of the roadways. Drive along the track takes about 30 mins.
Walking times: Pista de Lisier – Refugio de Lisier ¾ hr.; Refugio de Lisier – Es Montarruego 1¼ hrs.; Es Montarruego – Ibón de Ordizeto 1 hr.; return 2½ hrs.;

total time 5½ hrs.
Difference in height: 830m.
Grade: easy walk on GR path (marked red and white); lengthy stretch of roadway in the first part, afterwards a good path; only a few sections with a steep gradient. Take note: almost totally without shade.
Recommended map: Bachimala, 1:25,000; publ. by Editorial Alpina 2000.
Stops and accommodation: bars and restaurants in Plan.

The Ibón de Ordizeto can be reached from two sides: from Valle de Bielsa along a long and strenuous track or from the Valle de Chistau on an easy walk through the valleys Río Sallena and Río Montarruego. The wealth of scenic impressions along the way culminate in the marvellous view from the lake: you will rarely find such a wonderful view of the whole of the massif of Posets and Lardana.

The first stage of the walk begins at the **Pista de Lisier** with the GR 11 signpost. Along the gently ascending roadway you reach the Bordas de Lisier after half an hour. Cross a rivulet behind the houses and take the broad signposted path to the right immediately after that. Up a steep incline you come past the **Refugio de Lisier**, (self-catering hut for up to 6 people) 1740m, lying between trees on the left, and meet the forest track again. This brings you to a small col and then downhill again to the Barranco la Basa, on the way taking advantage of some shortcuts marked with cairns. Cross

Ibón de la Solana with the Posets massif in the background.

over the streambed and now gently climb up across grassy slopes round wide bends. The forest track ends at a little hut. Continue here along the path going straight ahead which crosses a slope on open ground after a wood and brings you closer to the Barranco de Montarruego to then change over onto the opposite side at a low point. Walk along beside the lively stream for a short way, then the path leaves the stream and ascends across the expansive hillside to a derelict shepherds' hut on a small rise which is a beautiful spot to stop and enjoy the view. You are now standing in the pretty side valley of **Es Montarruego**, 2060m, whose green mountain slopes are cut by torrents. The path turns southwards after the hut and ascends, partly in the eroded gullies, very quickly uphill to the long ridge which comes down from the Pico de las Tres Güegas. Just before the hilltop it turns to the west, runs across the slope on the level towards it and then changes over the ridge onto the other slope into the Barranco de Sallena. The path now crosses the long slope towards the clearly visible col, at first diagonally downhill, then again in an ascending straight line. After two or three zigzags you reach the Collado de Ordizeto at the track which comes up from the Valle de Bielsa. Follow the track left and after a few minutes you arrive at the **Ibón de Ordizeto**, 2370m. If you descend a few metres at the eastern dam of the lake, you find yourself standing above the small Ibón de la Solana – an especially beautiful viewpoint overlooking the Picos of Bachimala, Posets and Eriste.

39 Puerto de la Madera, 2525m

Delightful valleys in the area of famous three-thousanders

Campamento Virgen Blanca – Vado Bachimala – Puerto de la Madera and back

Location: Plan, 1120m
Starting point: Campamento Virgen Blanca, 1560m, about 8km along the track to Viadós, before the bridge over the Río Cinqueta de la Pez. Drive along the track takes about 35 mins.

You can drive further along the track as far as the Refugio de Tabernés (self-catering hut for 8 people), but it is in very bad condition. Drive past the Campamento, shortly afterwards past El Forcallo campsite, then the track branches off right to Viadós, straight on to the Refugio de Tabernés, 1730m. From there you walk down to the bridge over the Río Cinqueta de la Pez and take the wooded path waymarked in green on the other side; it ascends to a signposted crossroads where you meet the path from the Campamento.

Walking times: Campamento – Vado Bachimala 1 hr.; Vado Bachimala – Puerto de la Madera 2 hrs.; return 2½ hrs.; total time 5½ hrs.
Difference in height: 965 m.
Grade: easy, but long walk with considerable variation in height; altogether pleasant gradients. PR hiking trail (marked yellow and white).
Recommended map: Bachimala, 1:25,000; published by Editorial Alpina, 2000.
Stops and accommodation: bars and restaurants in Pla; bar in the El Forcallo campsite (only in summer).

Alternative: Puerto de la Pez, 2460m: varied landscape with delightful valley meadows, waterfalls, streams and slopes covered in flowers. At the fork in the Vado Bachimala cross over the stream on a little bridge further ahead and past a rain gauge on the right, keep heading for the steep slope on the right-hand side of the narrow cleft of the Gorgas de la Pez. The path gets steeper here, then runs through a thin pinewood mostly on the level and comes closer to the stream again. Past a Cabaña on the other bank of the stream you walk through the long valley plain and the climb up to the next hill begins after the Barranco Ibón de Bachimala which drops down from the right. After a short way along beside the stream you cross the Cinqueta de la Pez on some boulders (paint waymarkers on rocks), continue up the slope till you reach a platform at the end of which is the Puerto de la Pez. Not too high on the slopes, keep going towards the head of the valley with cairns here and there to help you find the way across the broad scree runs and gullies. The continuation of the path is clearly visible at the head of the valley: it continues up the scree slope, winds its way up to a band of rock, climbs across this and afterwards zigzags steeply uphill. Shortly below the top of the col it turns off right to the Puerto de la Pez. Difference in height: 900m, total time from Campamento, 6 hrs.

Wood was previously exported from the forests of Plan and San Juan into the French Vallée de Rioumajou over the Puerto de la Madera (wood pass) – today the border pass is a magnificent viewpoint for the famous massifs of Bachimala, Posets and Maladeta. This easy walk first leads through the delightful Valle de Tabernés with the Cinqueta de la Pez torrent, then across the wide rhododendron slopes of the Barranco de la Madera up to the pass.

At the **Campamento Virgen Blanca** take the yellow and white PR path before the bridge across the Río Cinqueta de la Pez which turns off left from the track. Quickly

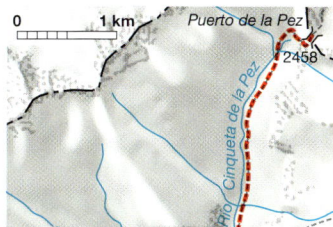

ascending at first, then more on the level, the broad forest path meets the track which you follow for a few minutes as far as the bridge over the Río Cinqueta de la Pez. Keep on this side, walk close to the stream to begin with, then across pasture slopes and through a pinewood. At a crossroads where the path coming from the Refugio de Tabernés joins, go straight on, cross the Barranco de Culrueba, ascend a small embankment, go past a Cabaña, and you approach the Cinqueta de la Pez.

The path goes along the bank of the stream and soon comes onto the broad valley plain of **Vado Bachimala**, 1800m. The path divides in the middle of the meadows: right is signposted to the Puerto de la Pez, but you turn left into the wood and now climb steeply up the hillside of the Barranco de la Madera. After half an hour you meet the old path used for the transportation of wood, follow it to the right and walk towards a small side stream before which you take a sharp bend to the left. Now ascend gently up across the slopes covered with many rhododendron bushes, proceed across a meadow ignoring a shortcut path veering off to the right, and you soon arrive at a small platform with the ruins of a hut. This beautiful place with a view of the mountains of the Valle de Gistaín is an ideal spot to stop for a rest. Now the path keeps heading westwards and runs across the slopes at

129

Open view of Bachimala.

a pleasant gradient. You reach the top round a few bends, then the Peña de Millarioux with its conspicuous covering of scree and below, the Puerto de la Madera comes into view; the broad col is divided by a hill. The path leads across the rock-splintered slopes and heads at first for the left-hand Collado to then branch off right before the slope going up to the col. Cross the col slopes cut by deep furrows and reach the spacious **Puerto de la Madera**, 2525m. From here it's a 10 minute climb up the small hill to the viewing point, 2581 m, on the left of the Puerto.

The return from here is easily accomplished over the south col. Tracks descend the slope of the col and come back to meet the ascent path.

In the valley of Río Cinqueta de la Pez.

40 Ibón de Millars, 2350m, and Ibón de Leners, 2520m

Two crystalline mountain lakes in high alpine surroundings

Refugio de Viadós – Plan de Las Tuertas – Ibón de Millars – Ibón de Leners and back

Location: Plan, 1120m.
Starting point: Refugio de Viadós, 1700m, at the end of the track from Plan to Viadós. Drive along the track takes about 45 minutes.
Walking times: Refugio de Viadós – Ibón de Millars 2¼ hrs.; Ibón de Millars – Ibón de Leners ½ hr.; return 2¼ hrs.; total time 5 hrs.
Difference in height: Ibón de Millars 650m; Ibón de Leners 820m.
Grade: in places steep and very loose scree sections of slope, otherwise a walk posing no problems; GR path as far as the fork at the Plan de Las Tuertas GR-Weg (waymarked red and white, alternative); cairns after that.
Recommended map: Bielsa-Val de Chistau, 1:40,000; published by Editorial Pirineo, 1998.
Refreshments: restaurants in Plan; bar at El Forcallo campsite (only in summer).
Tip: the Refugio de Viadós is a staffed hut with 70 overnight places; open from Easter week at weekends as well as through July and August. ℂ 974.50.60.82.

The group of peaks round the Pico Eriste form a beautiful and dramatic backdrop for several lakes above the Valle de La Rivereta. The Ibones de Millars and Leners are the largest of these, lying in deep hollows which have been ground out of the granite rock by former glaciers. On the walk from the green alpine slopes around Viadós into the landscape of lakes dominated by smoothly polished rock you often get a glimpse of chamois and, in the glass-clear waters, endemic salamanders (tritón pyrenaica).

At the end of the **Refugio de Viadós** track, cross the bridge over the Barranco de los Orieles and follow the GR path across meadow slopes past

The Ibón de Leners.

several barns as far as a fork with signposts. Turn off here right in the direction of Ibón de Millars, walk down to the Puente Palanca, change over onto the other bank of the Río Cinqueta and now walk downstream through the wood. The path soon leaves the stream and swings into the Valle de La Rivereta which you ascend on grassy slopes. After crossing a small stream gully, you come to junction. Go left here and at the top the path runs more on the level through a

pinewood. Past a spring on the left-hand side of the path you come to another gravel slope with a steep gradient and after a flat section through the wood the path now approaches the valley bottom. You can see ahead the water of the torrent cascading down through a gap in the rocks, dominated by a smooth slab of rock. Cross over the Barranco Las Tuertas coming in from the left and zigzag steeply up the bank on the other side. The wood gradually thins out and you reach the delightful high **Plan de Las Tuertas** valley, 2240m.

Go across the high plain as far as the signposts where the GR path continues straight on to the Collado de Eriste. Turn right over to the rocky hillside and climb up round some bends. After you have passed a tumble-down hut, you reach the ice-blue **Ibón de Millars**, 2350m. At the dry-stone wall change over onto the other side of the lake and follow the path marked with cairns. It leads through a pretty landscape of meadows, pools and light-coloured granite rock, sprinkled with spots of yellow lichen. The comfortably ascending path comes past derelict huts and finishes at the similarly dammed **Ibón de Leners**, 2520m.

41 Through Valle de Estós

Classic walk into one of the most beautiful valleys of the Parque Posets-Maladeta

Estós car park – Cabaña de Santa Ana – Cabaña del Turmo – Refugio de Estós and back

Location: Benasque, 1140m.
Starting point: Estós car park, 1300m. Drive from Benasque, after about 3km a signposted roadway turns off left straight after the Puente Nuevo de San Chaime. Car park after 500m.
Walking times: Estós car park – Cabaña de Santa Ana ¾ hr.; Cabaña de Santa Ana – Cabaña del Turmo 1¼ hrs.; Cabaña del Turmo – Refugio de Estós ½ hr.; return 2 hrs.; total time 4½ hrs.
Difference in height: 590m.
Grade: easy walk on GR path (marked red and white); roadway as far as the Cabaña del Turmo, a broader hiking trail after that. This 7km long walk ascends just under 600 vertical metres.
Recommended map: Valle de Benasque 1:30,000; published by Editorial Alpina 3000, 1999.
Stops and accommodation: bars and restaurants in Benasque; the Refugio de Estós is staffed all year round, 150 overnight places. Be sure to book ahead for meals and overnight stops, ✆ 974.55.14.83.

The Valle de Estós allows you access to many of the famous peaks, the ascent of which starts out from the Refugio. Perdiguero, Clarabide, Posets-Lardana are only some of the melodious names from the high alpine region of the three-thousanders. It forms a marvellous backdrop for this easy walk through a large valley with charming river pastures, rich grassy slopes, luxuriant mixed woods and the playful torrents of the Río de Estós.

The path into the Valle de Estós is signposted at the **car park**. After a short ascent you meet the roadway. Go left here and past the dam of the tiny

The Valle de Estós.

Embalse de Estós. Walk beside the Río de Estós, squeezed between the steep slopes, cross the river on a wooden bridge, go through a livestock gate (please close it again behind you!) and you come to the **Cabaña de Santa Ana**, 1540m. Walk leisurely through the expansive valley, in which there are endemic trees, firs, rowan trees, hazelnut trees, birch and beech trees. Past the splashing Fuente de Coronas on the left of the path you come to a fork where the Ibons de Batisielles are signposted (see Walk 42). Keep straight on, cross

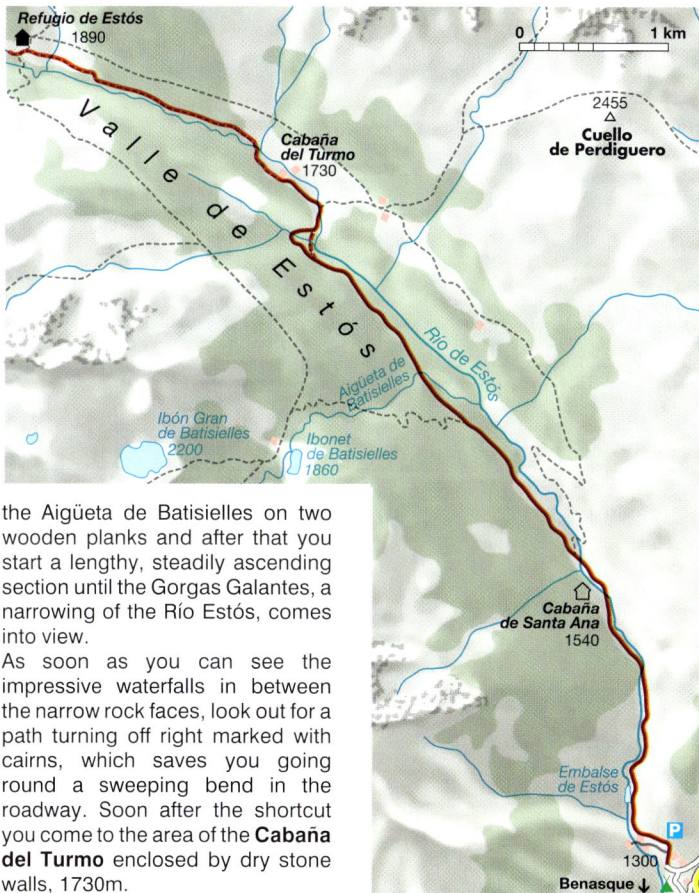

Refugio de Estós
1890

Cabaña del Turmo
1730

2455 △
Cuello de Perdiguero

Valle de Estós

Río de Estós

Aigüeta de Batisielles

Ibón Gran de Batisielles
2200

Ibonet de Batisielles
1860

Cabaña de Santa Ana
1540

Embalse de Estós

1300
Benasque ↓

0 ——— 1 km

the Aigüeta de Batisielles on two wooden planks and after that you start a lengthy, steadily ascending section until the Gorgas Galantes, a narrowing of the Río Estós, comes into view.

As soon as you can see the impressive waterfalls in between the narrow rock faces, look out for a path turning off right marked with cairns, which saves you going round a sweeping bend in the roadway. Soon after the shortcut you come to the area of the **Cabaña del Turmo** enclosed by dry stone walls, 1730m.

The road way ends here and your path continues to the left near the hut and leads through the bottom of the valley to a wooden bridge on which you change over onto the other side of Río Estós.

Eventually the path ascends the gentle hillside of the valley through a pinewood, then zigzags quickly up across open grassy slopes heading towards the **Refugio de Estós**, 1890m.

42 Ibón Gran de Batisielles, 2200m

An idyllic mountain lake with outstanding views

Estós car park – Cabaña de Santa Ana – Ibonet de Batisielles – Ibón Gran de Batisielles and back

The unique Maladeta massif.

Location: Benasque, 1140m.
Starting point: Estós car park. Drive from Benasque, after about 3km a signposted roadway branches off left straight after the Puente Nuevo de San Chaime. Car park after 500m.
Walking times: Estós car park – Cabaña de Santa Ana ¾ hr.; Cabaña de Santa Ana – Ibonet de Batisielles 1½ hrs.; Ibonet de Batisielles – Ibón de Batisielles 1 hr.; return 2¾ hrs.; total time 6 hrs.

Difference in height: 900m.
Grade: technically a straight forward walk along roadway as far as the fork in the Valle de Estós, then there are some sections of hefty uphill climbing in places; cairns.
Recommended map: Valle de Benasque 1:30,000; published by Editorial Alpina 3000, 1999.
Stops and accommodation: bars and restaurants in Benasque.

The Ibón Gran de Batisielles is one of many lakes in the high country of the western side of the Valle de Estós. The lake, as clear as glass in the middle of hilly pastures, is surrounded by steep rock walls and peaks with deep fissures. The distant view of the huge range of mountains in the north and the Maladeta massif in the west is magnificent.

The beginning of the walk is identical to the walk into the Valle de Estós (see Walk 41). At the fork after the **Cabaña de Santa Ana**, 1540m, follow the signpost for Ibonet de Batisielles. The broad path ascends up round long

bends through the wood, levels out and runs pretty well on the level as far as the Aigüeta de Batisielles. A little wooden bridge leads onto the other side of the stream and your path now continues round narrow bends through the wood, the gradient decreases and you reach a pretty meadow at the edge of the small **Ibonet de Batisielles**, 1860m. Just on the right of the pool can be found the tiny Cabaña de Batisielles and several signposted paths branch off in front of it. The path to the Ibón Gran de Batisielles leads left past the hut and immediately winds uphill with regular cairns to mark the way. The jagged peaks of the Cresta de Batisielles rise up ahead from which protrudes the peak of Tuca de Mincholet, split into enormous slabs. The other side of the Benasque valley is dominated by Maladeta and Aneto. Cross over a scree slope going off to the right and afterwards the path ascends steeply again and runs across grassy slopes and in between solitary granite boulders. Turn off to the left before a broad expanse of slope ascending high up further along the path. Continue up the gentle incline, across undulating grassy terrain towards the huge rock walls, at the foot of which lies the **Ibón Gran de Batisielles**, 2200m.

The Ibón Gran de Batisielles.

137

43 Valle de Remuñe, 2220m

Varied stroll through a peaceful side valley

End of the valley road – Ibonet de Remuñe – Ibones de Remuñe and back

Location: Benasque, 1140m.
Starting point: signpost about 250m before the end of the valley road, 1800m.
Walking times: valley road – Ibonet de Remuñe 1¾ hrs.; Ibonet de Remuñe – Ibones de Remuñe ½ hr.; return 1¾ hrs.; total time 4 hrs.
Difference in height: 420m.
Grade: this is an easy walk on marked paths (red waymarkings and cairns);

sure-footedness is absolutely essential since the terrain is strewn with boulders. The return via the Ibones de Remuñe demands some route-finding; but you can also walk back the way you came.
Recommended map: Valle de Benasque 1:30,000; published by Editorial Alpina 3000, 1999.
Stops and accommodation: bar and restaurant in Hospital de Benasque.

Only a few walkers stray into the northernmost side valley of the Valle de Benasque, perhaps because there are no spectacular mountains and backdrops here. In recompense, the walk though this valley, created by glaciers, offers a surprising diversity of scenery and makes for a wonderfully enjoyable experience. The return via the Ibones de Remuñe which lie in a hollow in the slope high above the valley, completes a grand day out.

Start the walk at a **signpost** for the Vall de Remuñe/Ibón de Remuñe on the left-hand side of the road by ascending up through a firebreak after which you walk through a park-like landscape with thin pinewoods, rhododendron bushes, granite boulders and branching rivulets. The mountain ridge of the pointed Tucas de Literola stands out ahead and you walk beside the steep granite slopes on your right that have been ground smooth by glaciers. As the path gently ascends you will see emerging ahead, a broad scree slope lying across the valley. The valley terrace is cut through by the Aigüeta de Remuñe on the left-hand side and your path climbs steeply up between the

The Ibonet de Remuñe.

barranco and the left-hand edge of the boulder field. After a good quarter of an hour you reach a plain, walk along the foot of rock debris on the right, then down to the stream which you then continue beside for a while. On the other side of the stream, the *barranco* is clearly visible which comes down from the Ibones de Remuñe and which you descend on the return. Ascend the hillside on the right, cross the inlet of a side stream then continue across rocky ground towards another terrace, this time cut through twice. The path moves away from the stream, ascends the hillside, keeps up along the top edge of a scree slope of light grey and rust-brown boulders, then reaches a plain with meadows where the shallow **Ibonet de Remuñe**, 2210m, lies at the foot of the steep valley wall on the right.

The path continuing to the Ibones de Remuñe is rather difficult to find at first. Orientate yourself towards the scree slope on the other side of the stream and keep heading for the cliffs bordering it on the left. Cross over the stream at some cairns and on the other side a marked path ascends the slope near the cliffs, turns eastwards further up and runs towards a solitary standing pine tree. You arrive at the smaller of the two lakes, continue along the left-hand bank and follow the cairns which lead you through a chaos of boulders to the plain situated a little higher with the large **Ibón de Remuñe**, 2220m. Follow the path here on the left-hand side of the lake as far as the outflow of the lake and descend the broad slope and rejoin the valley path.

44 Puerto de la Glera, 2360m

Beautiful mountain walk to the northernmost border pass of Valle de Benasque

End of the valley road – Ibón de Gorgutes – Puerto de la Glera and back

Location: Benasque, 1140m.
Starting point: end of the valley road, 1800m.
Walking times: valley road – Ibón de Gorgutes 2 hrs.; Ibón de Gorgutes – Puerto de la Glera ½ hr.; return 2 hrs.; total time 4½ hrs.
Difference in height: 560m.
Grade: easy walk on mule path waymarked in green; rather steep sections at the start. No shade at all along the way.
Recommended map: Valle de Benasque 1:30,000; published by Editorial Alpina 3000, 1999.
Stops and accommodation: bars and restaurants in Hospital de Benasque.

Like the Puerto de Benasque, the Puerto de la Glera was also once an important pass between the French town of Luchon and Benasque. Since the crossing of these high passes was very strenuous and exhausting especially in winter, easily accessible hostels were of significant importance for practicability. And so Hospice de Luchon was set up on the French side and Hospital de Benasque on the Spanish side. The ascent affords beautiful views over the valley and of the mountains of Maladeta and on the pass you can enjoy a wide panorama of the mountains around Luchon.

On the way to the Puerto de la Glera.

At the **end of the valley road** follow the signpost for Puerto de la Glera/Ibón de Gorgutes and the trail immediately climbs up between stunted pines to a grassy platform. After more uphill climbing you reach a small ledge with the

The Ibón de Gorgutes and the snow-covered Maladeta massif.

ruins of a hut. From here you have a beautiful view over the expansive valley of the Río Esera with pastures between Hospital de Benasque and La Besurta. At the end of the ledge the path swings to the west and winds up the south slope.

After a lengthy crossing of the slope in a northerly direction you come close to the Torrente de Gorgutes, walk beside it along its left-hand bank as far as a shallow ford where you cross the stream and then walk across a plain where the stream gently meanders. The route is unclear in places, but cairns indicate the direction towards the hillside ahead which you first climb diagonally to the north-east, then negotiate a few hairpin bends and afterwards keep going north-westwards again. Ascend a small rise, go past pools and round a southern foothill of the Pico de la Glera. You soon reach the **Ibón de Gorgutes**, 2320m, where the path continues along the right-hand side of the lake and cuts the slopes of the Pico de la Glera, strewn with boulders, which blocks the view of the pass right up until the last second. You then find yourself suddenly standing in front of the **Puerto de la Glera**, 2360m, by a little protecting wall.

45 Forau and Plan de Aiguallut, 2020m

Along the Sendero Geomorfológico to a unique and dramatic spectacle of nature

Hospital de Benasque – La Besurta – Forau de Aiguallut – Plan de Aiguallut and back

Location: Benasque, 1140m.
Starting point: Hospital de Benasque, 1740m. In summer you have to park just before the Hospital, 10 mins. along the road to the hotel buildings.
Walking times: Hospital de Benasque – La Besurta 1 hr.; La Besurta – Plan de Aigua-llut ¾ hr.; return 1½ hrs.; total time 3¼ hrs.
Difference in height: 280m.
Grade: easy walk on well-made PR path (marked yellow and white).
Recommended map: Valle de Benasque 1:30,000; published by Editorial Alpina 3000, 1999.
Stops and accommodation: bar and restaurant in Hospital de Benasque; bar at La Besurta car park (only in summer).
Tip: the walk can be shortened if you start at La Besurta. Although the drive to the car park there is closed in summer there's a shuttle bus between Hospital de Benasque and La Besurta. Timetable: daily from 8.00-21.30 at a maximum of half hourly intervals (as of summer 2001). Up-to-date information and timetables can be obtained from the tourist information in Benasque.

Alternative: Refugio and Collado de la Renclusa. At the fork you follow the signpost to the Refugio de la Renclusa and ascend wide hairpin bends to the platform with the Refugio. At the old hut turn to the left, came past some rain gauges on a hill and then climb up the left-hand edge of the slope through the wood in the direction of the col. The path keeps on the left of the streambed which is strewn with boulders further up and you reach the Collado de la Renclusa, 2270m, in half an hour.
From there continue along the flat col to the opposite hillside and go downhill round some bends. Descend the embankment in front of a tin bivouac to the Plan de Aiguallut. Walking time from the fork about 1½ hrs.
The Refugio de la Renclusa is staffed all year round; 110 overnight places (extended in 2001). Be sure to book ahead for meals and overnight stops, ℂ 974.55.14.90 or 974.55.21.06.

It is not without reason that the Plan de Aiguallut is the most popular place for an excursion in the Valle de Benasque. Wide meadows, stream meanders, waterfalls, the Maladeta massif, the Aneto glacier and of course, the dark Forau de Aiguallut, where the collected melt water suddenly disappears and flows underground and eventually feeds the Garonne in the Val d'Arán – all that combines into a wonderful nature experience which you will want to take your time to enjoy. You will hardly meet a soul as far as La Besurta, but the path is very heavily used from there onwards to the Plan de Aiguallut in summer.
The path begins at **Hospital de Benasque** on the left of the hotel buildings at some signposts. Cross the stream on the bridge, then keep heading towards the enclosed pastureland through the bottom of the valley, walk

Information board for the Sendero Geomorfológico.

along beside the dry stone walls and cross the stream again, this time on some logs. A little further on the path divides: follow the path in the direction of Besurta/Forau de Aiguullaut and now ascend the hillside leisurely up

La Basurta pastures.

round some bends. The gradient decreases after 10 minutes and you walk through the wood and come to an information board for the Sendero Geomorfológico: on the other side of the valley you can see the Canal de Aludes de Paderna, a broad break through the otherwise densely wooded slopes which has been formed by the regular avalanche waste from the Paderna peaks.

Now continue your walk and stroll through a narrow little side valley separated from the main stream with deep green marshy meadows and a thin pinewood as far as the start of the expansive valley floor of the Plan d'Están. A second board provides information about the valley basin covered by a lake after the retreat of the glaciers which has been gradually filled up with rock and sand; today a lake only forms periodically after extensive rainfall, otherwise only one or two pools are to be seen.

The path now runs above the valley pastures, comes to a fork which leads on further left to the Puerto de la Picada, but you keep right and walk down to the valley plain to reach the road. Go left here, past a *refugio* with a round tin roof, then a wooden post with yellow and white waymarkings points right

Forau de Aiguallut: unique natural spectacle.

to a path taking you on a shortcut across the bend in the road and quickly ascends up to the small rise where the car park of **La Besurta** is situated, 1890m. After the wooden bridge follow the broad path, cross a streambed and come along the partly 'paved' path to a junction. Straight on goes on to the Refugio de la Renclusa (see Aternative) which is the starting point for the high alpine ascents up Aneto and Maladeta, but you take the path on the left, now waymarked in green, climb a small rise and continue there on a level path across the valley hillside.

Another slight incline, then you are standing at the wooden barrier of the deep **Forau de Aiguallut**, 2000m, which gathers all the water from the nearby cascades. There are only a few minutes remaining after the information board about the subterranean drainage system before the path reaches the wide meadows of the **Plan de Aiguallut**, 2020m, where you make a pleasurable stop with the Aneto glacier providing a splendid backdrop.

46 Puerto de la Picada, 2480m, and Tuc dera Escaleta, 2465m

Walk along the pass on an old bridle path with spectacular panoramas

Refugio de Plan d'Están – Puerto de la Picada – Coth de Lunfèrn – Tuc dera Escaleta and back

Location: Benasque, 1140m.
Starting point: road to La Besurta, shortly after the Refugio de Plan d'Èstán, 1860m. From Hospital de Benasque drive along the surfaced road in the direction of La Besurta, the refugio (round tin roof) lies on the right-hand side after the bridge across the Río Ésera, shortly afterwards there's a signpost on the left of the road where you can park.
Walking times: car park – Puerto de la Picada 1½ hrs.; Puerto de la Picada -Tuc dera Escaleta ½ hrs.; return 1½ hrs.; total time 3½ hrs.
Difference in height: 620m.
Grade: easy walk on well-trodden paths with slight gradients. No shade.

Recommended map: Valle de Benasque 1:30,000; published by Editorial Alpina 3000, 1999.
Stops and accommodation: bar and restaurant in Hospital de Benasque; bar at the La Besurta car park (only in summer).
Tip: the drive to La Besurta is closed off in summer. There's a shuttle bus from Hospital de Benasque (for information see 'Getting there'). From the car park in La Besurta walk for a quarter of an hour along the yellow and white marked path down to the river plain and cross this to the signpost on the road.
Alternatively you can walk from Hospital de Benasque to the starting point (see Walk 45).

The untaxing and quick ascent to the Puerto de la Picada is nevertheless not short of magnificent views of the many-faceted landscapes around Benasque. And so the surprise when you stand on the rounded 'summit' of the Tuc dera Escaleta is even more impressive – an infinite wide view across the French mountains, the mountain chains Val d'Aran, the view back of the precipitous and fissured range of peaks of the mountains along the border and above them all, the glaciers and peaks of the Maladeta massif.

On the way to the Puerto de la Picada.

Your first objective, the Puerto de la Picada, is indicated at the **signposts** at the edge of the road. Follow the path going up the hillside that soon becomes wide sweeping bends round which you gain height up a steady pleasant incline. After a series of shorter hairpin bends they get longer again. Ignore a cart track turning off right in the meantime. The continuation of your path is indicated at an obvious junction by a wooden

post waymarked in red (Ruta hipica). Take this right-hand turn-off and meet the old path again on a bend higher up which you finally leave to the right along the path waymarked once more with a wooden post. Now walk leisurely across grassy slopes with well-established granite boulders, pass close to a pool (a few paces further on two pools lie on the left below on a sloping plateau) and turn towards the slope up to the Puerto. After the gentle ascent you reach the **Puerto de la Picada**, 2480m. A hump-backed platform spreads out below with mini pools and is flanked in the south-west by sheer rocks.

On the hillside path on the left, walk down to a small col with several signposts and there follow the direction to Cloth de Lunfèrn. There's a short section on the right along the jagged ridge, then the path changes at the **Cloth de Lunfèrn**, 2400m, onto the left-hand side of the slope and forks immediately afterwards. The well-trodden path to the left descends to the Còth dera Monjòia, but you stay on the grassy path straight ahead and ascend the elongated ridge as far as the rounded summit of the **Tuc dera Escaleta**, 2465m, where a fantastic view awaits you.

At the Puerto de la Picada.

47 Coll de Toro and Ibón de Toro, 2235m

A charming high valley and a pass above the Vall d'Aran with beautiful views

La Besurta – Ibón de Toro and back

Location: Benasque, 1140m.
Starting point: La Besurta, 1890m.
Walking times: La Besurta – Ibón de Toro 1¾ hrs.; return 1½ hrs.; total time 3¼ hrs.
Difference in height: 345 m.
Grade: mostly leisurely paths; altogether pleasant gradients. No shade.
Recommended map: Valle de Benasque 1:30,000 published by Editorial Alpina 3000, 1999.

Stops and accommodation: bar and restaurant in Hospital de Benasque, bar at the car park in La Basurta (only in summer).
Tip: the drive to La Basurta is closed in summer. From Hospital de Benasque there's a shuttle bus (see information on 'Getting there'.) Alternatively you can walk from Hospital de Benasque to the starting point (see Walk 45).

You can appreciate this walk with the varied facets of a high valley which is characterised by streams and lakes, light-coloured granite rock, green meadows and slopes and the towering peaks around the Tuca de Mulleres. From the Ibón de Toro lying in a hollow of the broad ridge of the col, there's a beautiful view over the Val d'Aráncan.

Follow Walk 45 from **La Besurta** as far as the Plan de Aiguallut. When you arrive there, stay on the path which runs through the meadow plain on the left at the edge of the hillside and then divides at a signpost. Barrancs is signposted to the right there and straight on, the Coll de Toro. Follow the path waymarked with a cairn and keep heading through stony grassland

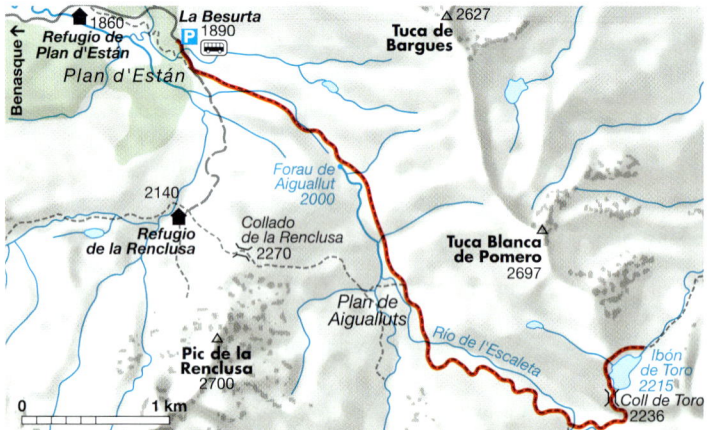

The Ibón de Toro.

straight for the Río de l'Escaleta which runs along on the left of the valley plain. Change over onto the other side of the stream and go uphill round some short bends. The path divides into many dirt paths on the ridge which all lead through the beautiful valley of the Río de l'Escaleta more or less close to the stream. The glacier-shaped granite thresholds of the valley hillsides and the limestone funnels in the ground you walk past, show really clearly how various types of rock butt against one another. The peaks of Tucas de Mulleres rise up clearly ahead and they close off the Escaleta valley from the neighbouring one of Val d'Aran. Walk towards the head of the valley along the comfortable path, but do not follow the stream branching off to the right which flows down from the Ibones de la Escaleta situated on the higher ledges, keep straight on for the time being at the foot of the long slope on your left-hand side. Then the path ascends the slope, goes round a sharp bend and runs up to the Coll de Toro. The lake lies a few metres below in a trough, embedded between the scree-covered hillsides of the Peña Nera and Malh dera Artiga, and the pass on the opposite side opens out into the Val d'Aran.

In a few minutes you come down to the **Ibón de Toro**, 2215m where you walk along the scree-covered bank on the left of the lake in a quarter of an hour over to the other side of the col where a splendid view across the neighbouring valley awaits you.

48 Pico de Paderna, 2620m

A panoramic view of spectacular mountain landscapes

La Besurta – Refugio de la Renclusa – Collado de Paderna – Pico de Paderna and back

Location: Benasque, 1140m.
Starting point: La Besurta car park, 1890m.
Walking times: La Besurta – Refugio de la Renclusa ¾ hr.; Refugio de la Renclusa – Collado de Paderna 1½ hrs.; Collado de Paderna – Pico de Paderna ½ hr.; return 2¼ hrs.; total time 5 hrs.
Difference in height: 730m.
Grade: moderate walk on leisurely paths to the Ibón de la Renclusa, paths from then on are mostly obvious. Really strenuous, at times steep gradient up to the Collado de Paderna and in the summit area. Sure-footedness essential as you cross a boulder field.
Recommended map: Valle de Benasque

1:30,000; published by Editorial Alpina 3000, 1999.
Stops and accommodation: bar and restaurant in Hospital de Benasque; bar at La Besurta car park (only in summer). The Refugio de la Renclusa is staffed all year round; 110 overnight places.
Be sure to book ahead for meals and overnight stops, ℂ 974 55 14 90; 974 55 21 06.
Tip: the drive to La Besurta is closed off in summer. There's a shuttle bus from Hospital de Benasque (see information on ' Getting there').
Alternatively you can walk from Hospital de Benasque to the starting point (see Walk 45).

The steep walled 'Tres Hermanas de Paderna' in the north-western extension of the Maladeta massif do not seem, on first view, to be easily accessible. But one of the 'Three sisters', the Pico de Paderna, can be climbed along the south ridge and affords a spectacular view of the neighbouring peaks and the glaciers of Maladeta. The way there through the idyllic valley of the Torrente de Alba puts you in the right mood for the summit experience.

At **La Besurta** car park follow the signposted path to the Refugio de la

Renclusa. After the wooden bridge across the stream the yellow and white marked path leads you through a pretty valley plain, crosses a mostly dry streambed and ascends gradually as far as a fork with signposts. The path to the left continues to the Forau de Aiguallut (see Walk 45), but you keep straight ahead and ascend along the left-hand edge of the slope through lots of rhododendrons along the comfortable zigzag path frequently paved with natural stone, which brings you directly to the **Refugio de la Renclusa**, 2140m. A path on the other side of the hut leads down to the Barranco de la Renclusa, where you cross the stream on two little bridges, climb upstream on the right-hand bank and approach the Torrente d'Alba flowing from the east which brings water down from the Ibones de la Renclusa situated higher up. The dirt path, more like a furrow, keeps on the right of the stream and energetically ascends

The 'sisters' of Pico de Paderna.

the slope densely covered in rhododendrons. Soon the path levels out and you walk along the bank of the babbling stream and look for a suitable place to change over onto the path which runs along on the other side. Follow the path through this idyllic high valley with its meandering stream, come to the small Ibón de la Renclusa (the larger Ibón lies above the path on the left to which you can make a detour in just a few minutes) and keep heading towards the valley floor strewn with big boulders in the south-west. Cairns guide you through the boulder field where you need to take care when climbing over the large blocks of granite. A plain covered in a moraine of debris stretches out in front of you and on the right-hand side you can see a very steep gravel slope which runs down from the Collado de Paderna. Avoid the extremely exhausting direct ascent and following the cairns, walk towards the streambed, cross immediately over the stream and start up the strenuous incline. You soon cross the stream again and now climb uphill on the left of it round some narrow bends. At a cliff the clearly marked path turns to the south-west, goes round a sheer slab of granite, then swings to the west and zigzags steeply up the hillside. The long Paderna ridge is clearly visible from here. Then the path turns sharply to the north and heads straight for the line of the ridge and the two sisters of Pico de Paderna rise up unexpectedly on the left – their rock masses constructed in vertical parallel layers seem much more precipitous and uniformly sheer. From now on the path descends and flanks the left-hand side of the ridge until you reach the **Collado de Paderna**, 2505m.

Go uphill again from here, at first really steeply up across the mountain slope on the left below the ridge, then along the narrow ridge as far as **Pico de Paderna**, 2620m, with summit signs. If you would like to complete the dazzling view, you can reach the small pre-summit of Paderna along the short narrow ridge.

49 Ibones de Vallibierna, 2480m

Diverse scenery in the area of the Maladeta massif

Refugio de Coronas – Pleta de Llosars – Ibones de Vallibierna

Location: Benasque, 1140m.
Starting point: Refugio de Coronas, 1950m (self-catering hut, space for 20 people, emergency telephone), at the end of the 9km long roadway from La Senarta through the Valle de Vallibierna.
Drive along the track takes about 30 minutes.
Walking times: Refugio de Coronas – Pleta de Llosars ¾ hr.; Pleta de Llosars – Ibón Bajo de Vallibierna ¾ hr.; Ibón Bajo de Vallibierna – Ibón Alto de Vallibierna ½ hr.; retour 1¾ hrs.; in total 3¾ hrs.
Difference in height: 530m.

Grade: easy walk on GR path (marked red and white). Only a few rather steep sections; the route between the two lakes runs frequently over granite boulders.
Recommended map: Valle de Benasque, 1:30,000; published by Editorial Alpina 3000, 1999.
Stops and accommodation: bars and restaurants in Benasque.
Tip: the roadway into the Valle de Vallibierna is closed off in summer. There's a regular shuttle bus between Plan de Senarte ad Refugio de Coronas (see information on 'Getting there').

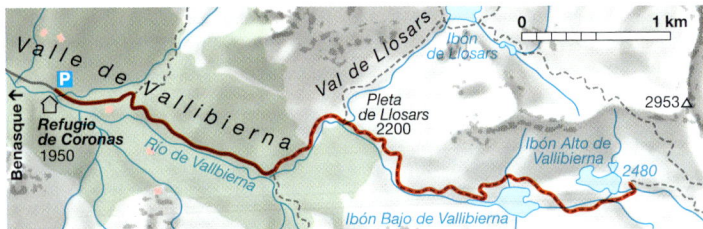

The smoothly polished granite and the eroded terraces with countless lakes, are evidence of the glaciation of the Valle de Vallibierna in the ice-age. The valley is bordered in the north by the chain of peaks of the big three-thousanders with Pico de Aneto as the centrepiece and in the south by the moderate range of mountains of the Sierra Negra. Scree slopes, forests, meadows of flowers, streams, clear mountain lakes and of course the imposing backdrop of mountains make this valley a popular objective. On the walk to the Ibones de Vallibierna at the eastern end of the valley a beautiful and contrasting landscape is displayed from all sides.
At the **Refugio de Coronas** follow the signs for the Ibones de Vallibierna, cross the side stream and walk along the stony roadway through the valley bottom. At the end of this the path turns off right, gets narrower and ascends up through the valley of the Río de Vallibierna. The huge Tuca de Vallibierna rises up ahead on the right. The path gets broader and quickly runs up the sloping ledge to the higher terrace, the **Pleta de Llosars**, 2200m. The pretty

edge of the valley with flat marshy meadows and a meandering stream is cut off in the north-east by smooth granite walls above which rise the jagged foothills of the Maladeta massif.

Your path divides here and you continue straight on to the Ibón de Llosars, then immediately right, across the stream on some stones. (If the stream is too full of water you have to walk to the end of the meadow and cross over there.) Follow the red and white marked path on the other side and ascend up between granite slabs in a south-easterly direction. You are getting close to the Barranco de Vallibierna, cross the stream and now go uphill on the left-hand bank as far as the small col behind which there's broad rock corridor. The stream flows down through this from the Ibón Bajo de Vallibierna.

Further along the path on the left-hand bank you come to the actual lake in a few minutes, keep on its left-hand side, ascend the slope to get round the steep rocky bank and walk above the lake to the end of it. The path there descends to a streambed strewn with boulders, crosses the boulders with the aid of cairns (the red and white waymarkings are rather feint) and then climbs up the conspicuous knoll and changes over onto the other side further up. The path then makes its way across the boulder-strewn slope down to the valley floor similarly strewn with large blocks of granite, continues across the boulders and later becomes a dirt path bringing you to the **Ibón Alto de Vallibierna**, 2480.

Taking a break on the Pieta de Llosars.

50 Lake walk in the south-eastern part of the Posets Maladeta nature reserve

A round walk through unspoilt mountain scenery with numerous glacial lakes

Estany de Llauset – Estany de Botornás – Estany de Cap de Llauset – Estanyets de Cap d'Anglos – Estany de Llauset

Location: Vilaller, 980m.
Starting point: car park at Estany de Llauset, 2195m. Drive to the reservoir along an asphalt road from Aneto; the village lies on the N-230 north of Vilaller.
Walking times: car park – Estany de Botornás ¾ hr.; Estany de Botornás – Estany de Cap de Llauset 1 hr.; Estany de Cap de Llauset – Estanyets de Cap d'Anglos 1 hr.; Estanyets de Cap d'Anglos – car park 1 hr.; total time 3¾ hrs.
Difference in height: 485m (including ascent up to the Collado d'Anglos).
Grade: technically easy walk on mostly leisurely GR path, marked red and white; many paths go across granite boulders, the ascents and descents of the *collados*

are short, but steep in places.
Recommended map: Alta Ribagorça (Mapa comarcal de Catalunya), 1:50,000; published by Institut Cartogràfic de Catalunya, 1995.
Stops and accommodation: bars and restaurants in Vilaller.
Tip: the drive to the car park at the Llauset reservoir is, at the end, through a long tunnel that is normally open. You do not need to worry about a warning sign at the entrance. If the tunnel is closed off, you will have to park a few bends lower down near some buildings and there take the signposted Senda Llauset GR (marked red and white). An additional 2 hrs. there and back.

The Montanuy section of the Parque Posets-Maladeta forms a small natural museum about the intensive work of a glacier. At various altitudes in the valley the ice flows have eroded hollows and basins which hold crystal clear lakes. These characterise the landscape together with the large morainal fields of polished granite boulders and the abrupt and fissured mountain flanks.

Go through the short tunnel at the car park at **Estany de Llauset** and the round walk begins at the signpost after that. First head towards the Estany de Botornás. The path is stabilised all the way to the end above the large reservoir where it turns off to the right and curves up across the northern slope. Shortly after a derelict hut you come past a large cairn where the path continues northwards through granite boulders. The **Estany de Botornás**, 2345m, comes into view below. The path again goes across piles of boulders on the right of the lake, then you walk beside the little stream which flows to the lake along the slowly ascending path. After crossing the stream go across an area of rubble again and at the following fork orientate yourself in the direction of Anglios/Estany de Cap de Llauset, so continue straight ahead and down to the stream where the path keeps close to the bank for a while and then crosses over onto the other side. The path starts up an incline there, bends round to the right and reaches the valley hollow further up with the **Estany de Cap de Llauset**, 2460m. Keep on the right-hand bank as far as the end of the lake

Estany de Botornás.

and climb the Collet dels Estanyets along the path as it leads over boulders once more. There's a beautiful view on the col of the enormous Pico de Vallibierna and its neighbouring peaks in the west, as well as the mountain ranges of Aigües-Tortes in the east. The small Anglos lakes lie one after the other in the narrow valley below and the twisting descent down the hillside is somewhat steep and a bit slippery sometimes. When you have reached the valley at the **Estanyets de Cap d'Anglos** (2340m) stay on the now level path on the right of the series of lakes, in between times climbing over boulders. Further ahead the valley opens up into a plain of lakes and the path runs towards a wooden shepherds' hut, the Refugio d'Anglos. The path divides about 100m in front of it and there are waymarkings on the rock. Straight on past the *refugio* you come into the Salenques valley and the walk continues to the right in the direction of Llauset (white waymarkings). Up a moderate incline keep on the left of the Estany de l'Obaga where the waymarkings are mostly rather confusing. After a short flat section the path bends to the left onto the south-western slope (look out for the red and white waymarkers). The animal tracks which lead straight ahead can be deceiving at this point! The path winds up the steep slope to the Collado d'Anglos. The Estany de Llauset lies below and some swift bends take you down the steep incline to the lake where some short precipitous sections are made safe with a handrail. There are some cement steps at the end and you come back to the signpost at the beginning of the walk.

Index